©2010 Mary Bell, Heidi Dybing, Nancy Martinson, Jennifer Wood

Printed on recycled paper with soy-based ink in the United States of America

The Dry Store Publishing Company
28097 Goodview Drive
Lanesboro, MN 55949
marytbell@drystore.com
FAX 507-467-2694

All the energy it took to put this book together was given by the generous and thoughtful members of our community. The whole thing - kit and kaboodle - was a communtiy effort. Profits from this book will go to an endowment fund to perpetuate the Rhubarb Festival.

www.rhubarbfestival.org

Everything Rhubarb: Recipes and Stories from a Small Town that Celebrates Rhubarb / Mary Bell, Heidi Dybing, Nancy Martinson, Jennifer Wood

Includes Index
ISBN 978-0- 9653572-7-2
Library of Congress Control Number: 2010924857

First Edition
 2 3 4 5 6 7 8 9 10 11 12 13 14 15 16 17 18 19 20

Editors: Jennifer Wood, Maggie Molyneaux
Illustrators: Judy Smithson, Leisa Luis-Grill, Joan Finnegan
Photographs: Joe Deden, Renee Bergstrom, Marvin Eggert, Frank Wright, Lisa Brainard

Cover Design: Ira Newman
Researchers: Frank Wright, Pam Niven

Everything Rhubarb

Recipes and Stories from a Small Town that Celebrates Rhubarb

Top Stalk
Nancy Martinson

The Root
Heidi Dybing

Tallest Stalk
Mary Bell

Newest Stalk
Jennifer Wood

Introduction

Books usually have one or possibly two authors, but our book, Everything Rhubarb is different. It's about rhubarb and community and was put together by the Divine Rhubarb Committee, Mary Bell, Heidi Dybing, Nancy Martinson and Jennifer Wood. We all felt the call to create the rhubarb festival and to document it.

Nancy Martinson is the self-appointed Top Stalk. "I'm the organizer, the one who keeps all the balls in the air and makes sure that everything gets done and everyone is in the right place to make the Rhubarb Festival work. When I wrote the letter to Garrison Keillor I had no title and our organization had no official name, so I decided to be the Top Stalk and call us the Divine Rhubarb Committee. It was that easy!"

Mary Bell believes that rhubarb is the perfect plant. "You plant it once, and then year after year, with minimal attention it produces an abundant supply of food. I call it the giving plant. I have over 125 rhubarb plants that I use to make and dry a rhubarb sauce that children love, especially my grandkids Hunter and Alysse"

"After Nancy and Mary hatched the idea of a Rhubarb Festival, they needed a partner to do the "root" work of painting signs, sewing banners and inventorying supplies," says Heidi Dybing. "That's who I am . . . the root."

Jennifer Wood is relatively new to Lanesboro and the most recent member of the committee. "It all started innocently enough . . . I simply asked when there would be a book with recipes from the rhubarb tasting contest! I came in handy as this book became a reality."

Acknowledgements

While putting this book together we kept a list of the people we wanted to thank. We soon realized that the list would include more than half the town of Lanesboro. This book is a reflection of individuals who play multiple roles within this community - all the mothers, brothers, fathers, sisters, aunties, uncles, children, grandchildren, nieces, nephews, in-laws, out-laws, friends, neighbors, husbands, wives and ex's who gave of themselves to make this book happen. Hope we didn't forget anyone.

Thank you!

Foreword

When I think about the things in life that bring us together, where people gather and stand or sit and talk awhile and share their lives, or just kick back in silence in the midst of it all, what comes to mind are really very simple things: water, fire, weddings, funerals, and family reunions. And storms. And, if you've wandered through the Root River Valley in Southeastern Minnesota in the springtime of the year, it's rhubarb.

I don't recall the first time I tasted rhubarb, but I do remember the last. It was here in this valley, in Lanesboro, at a festival put on by The Divine Rhubarb Committee and a host of other volunteers, where people from all around come to enjoy rhubarb and the people who grow it and cook with it and want nothing more than to share it and a bit of hospitality with anyone who cares to drop by.

There are people who've got rhubarb plants in their yards dating back a hundred years or more. It's a hardy plant, a ruddy plant, a plant that's both practical and versatile, yet humble and unassuming. It can be shared; if you don't have any, just say the word and someone will leave some on your porch. Juiced, sauced, pied or dried – it simply tastes good.

When you visit Lanesboro, you'll find a Farmer's Market with cookies and bars, pies and tarts, preserves and salsas and breads – all made with rhubarb. But it isn't the rhubarb alone that will bring you back; it's the spirit of community, the feeling you get from being around people who know about working together for the common good. It's the heart and soul of this small town, and the blessing is you take it with you when you go. That and a little book chock full of rhubarb recipes, and a jar or two of rhubarb sauce, just right with buttermilk biscuits and coffee. You'll want to invite a friend or two, of course. Rhubarb has that effect on a person.

Mrs. Sundberg

You'll find Mrs. Sundberg's thoughts featured weekly on prairiehome.org.

Table of Contents

Lanesboro: Our Small Town

On April 22, 2008, Lanesboro, Minnesota became "The Rhubarb Capital of Minnesota" by state proclamation.

The town of Lanesboro is surrounded by limestone bluffs and tucked in the scenic Root River valley of southeastern Minnesota.

The steep slopes, deep valleys, rolling fields, historic buildings, Victorian homes and 60-mile paved bike trail that hugs the river make Lanesboro a popular destination. It's home to about 800 residents.

Mother Earth News recognized Lanesboro on the 2009 "Great Places You've (Maybe) Never Heard Of" list honoring the city's cultural and natural attractions.

Settled by Irish Catholics and Norwegian Lutherans, the town was established by the Lanesboro Land Company in 1868 as a destination for Eastern vacationers. Although still attracting visitors from far and wide, Lanesboro is often referred to as "the best kept secret in the Midwest."

Over the hill from downtown Lanesboro is Eagle Bluff Environmental Learning Center, a vital residential educational campus in the midst of thousands of acres of state hardwood forestland. This magical place provides great hiking, birding and hunting opportunities.

The Root River Watershed, long known for its first-class trout fishing, has become a playground for those who canoe, kayak, float and camp. Karst geology and the watershed have carved deep caves, numerous sinkholes and underground streams.

Lanesboro was named one of America's Prettiest Towns in 2010 by Yahoo! Travel / Forbes Traveler for scenic beauty and small town charm.

Minnesota, land of 11,842 lakes does not have one named "Rhubarb Lake."

In 2009 Lanesboro became "The Bed & Breakfast Capital of Minnesota."

Downtown Lanesboro has many original buildings that offer eating and shopping opportunities; from ice cream and fine dining to local artisan goods.

Within this vibrant agricultural and tourism community we are proud of the diversity of cultural experiences provided by the Commonweal Theater Company and the Lanesboro Arts Center.

Around 1,000 dairy farms still thrive in a five-county southeastern Minnesota area.

Fillmore County raises more beef cattle than any other county in Minnesota.

Lanesboro is home to one of the last three sales barns left in Minnesota. On Wednesdays and Fridays there is a steady parade of livestock trailers in and out of town.

Vision for our county: everyone has at least one rhubarb plant.

Starting in April and running until October on Wednesday afternoons and Saturday mornings the Lanesboro Farmer's Market comes to life. Amish buggies trot past the impressive dam and waterfall and join with the local Farmer's Market vendors at Sylvan Park to sell plants, seasonal garden vegetables, a variety of locally grown fruit, homemade bread, jelly, jam, homegrown shiitake mushrooms, eggs, chicken, beef, pork, a selection of dried foods and much more.

Throughout the season vendors bring watercress, ramps, blackcaps, morel mushrooms, maple syrup, honey black walnuts, ginseng and, of course, rhubarb.

Our town is increasingly becoming known as a local food destination where everyone is encouraged to live locally, live well and find ways to support one another.

The Rhubarb Festival is one way people work and play together to strengthen the fabric of community.

A vision for southeastern Minnesota is to become known as a food destination with a mushroom festival, tomato festival, chard festival, squash festival - and more?

7

A house resolution

recognizing Lanesboro as the rhubarb capital of Minnesota

WHEREAS, our state is enhanced by the presence of those communities with unique cultural activities that are deserving of special legislative recognition; and

WHEREAS, rhubarb and the citizens of Lanesboro are both versatile and reliable; and

WHEREAS, rhubarb and Lanesboro burst forth with new life and energy every spring; and

WHEREAS, Lanesboro has elevated the status of rhubarb from undervalued and underutilized to appreciated and desirable; and

WHEREAS, rhubarb wine has been made in Lanesboro's Scenic Valley Winery for over a decade; and

WHEREAS, Lanesboro started an annual Rhubarb Festival three years ago to help promote the Lanesboro Farmers Market and to celebrate all that is rhubarb; and

WHEREAS, this year's festival will be held on June 7, 2008, from 10 a.m. to 2 p.m. at Sylvan Park; and

8

WHEREAS, there will be contests and prizes for largest rhubarb leaf and heaviest rhubarb stalk, People's Choice awards for best-tasting rhubarb pies, crisps, cakes, soups, chutneys, chili, jams, ketchup, and drinks; and

WHEREAS, Lanesboro has the only Rhubarb Olympics in the state of Minnesota; and

WHEREAS, the Rhubarb Olympics will include the rhubarb stalk throw, rhubarb golf, green eggs and rhubarb, rhubarb hoops, and rhubarb toss, and have categories for kids and adults; NOW, THEREFORE,

BE IT RESOLVED by the Committee on Rules and Legislative Administration of the House of Representatives of the State of Minnesota that it recognizes Lanesboro as the rhubarb capital of Minnesota.

Dated: April 22, 2008

Margaret Anderson Kelliher, Speaker
Minnesota House of Representatives

Anthony "Tony" Sertich, Chair
Rules and Legislative Administration

Ken Tschumper
State Representative

9

The Festival

Every year on the first Saturday of June rhubarb becomes the center of everyone's attention at our Rhubarb Festival in Sylvan Park . . . and you are invited. If you can't come, this book will bring the festival to you with our collection of favorite recipes, pictures and stories from the rhubarb-filled events.

Sylvan Park stretches over two city blocks and at festival time a leafy green canopy shades picnic tables, shelters, a gazebo, a playground, a camping area and two small trout ponds.

Just after sunrise dozens of volunteers stream into the park, eager to help get everything ready. Workers pound stakes in the ground to section off areas for the Rhubarb Olympics. Banners and signs go up. Clotheslines are strung from tree to tree for aprons to blow freely in the wind and decorate the park. The stage is assembled and the sound system is put to the test. Tables are arranged in the gazebo where volunteer servers put on their aprons and spread homemade tablecloths to prepare for the main event - the taste testing of everything rhubarb.

Meanwhile the Farmer's Market vendors are arranging their booths to showcase rhubarb. Members of various civic and church groups take

over the shelters to sell their rhubarb offerings to raise funds for their organizations. One of the groups, the Bethlehem Youth, prepares for a swift business of selling Rhu-dogs, which are hotdogs on toasted buns smothered with rhubarb ketchup.   Soon the parade of rhubarb enthusiasts, armed with trays, bowls, slow cookers and coolers start to arrive with their rhubarb concoctions for the tasting contest.

Every year two local television celebrities, Ted Schmidt and Jess Abrahamson, vigorously toss the first stalk of rhubarb to get the Rhubarb Olympics underway.

The festival officially begins when The Rhubarb Sisters take the stage and belt out our Rhubarb National Anthem.

Beth Hennessy, one of the original Rhubarb Sisters, wrote the words to the Anthem and most of the other songs in the Sisters' repertoire.

Rhubarb National Anthem

O beautiful for rhubarb stalks,
For red and green and pink,
For lovely green expansive leaves
Above the kitchen sink.

Oh, rhubarb plant, oh, rhubarb plant,
God shed his grace on thee,
And crown thy good and darling would
You share your recipe?

The Anthem is a parody of America the Beautiful. Original lyrics (1893) by Katharine Lee Bates, first appeared in print on July 4, 1895. These new words were written by Beth Hennessy for The Rhubarb Sisters.

Tom Barnes, Tim Kiehne and Peter Torkelson, our local rhubarb jugglers, ignite stalks of rhubarb and toss the flaming rhubarb back and forth for the appreciative crowd.

"It's the Stalk! " Based on "It's the Girl," with original words by Dave Oppenheim, 1931. Parody by Beth Hennessy, 2009.

It's the Stalk!

Some folks want atmosphere in Lanesboro town,
They say the trail and river make life grand.
I've got my own ideas pertaining to this,
Just listen to this song, you'll understand.

It isn't the paddle, it's not the canoe,
It isn't the bike trail or cows that say "moo",
It isn't the great views that bring joy to you,
It's the stalk! It's the stalk!

It isn't the great shops that you wander to,
It isn't theatre, or art that is new,
It isn't the restaurants, the food or the brew,
It's the stalk! It's the stalk!

Even tho' we know some folks may doubt it;
Here is our small town we celebrate it.

It isn't the songbirds, the songs that they sing;
It isn't the sunshine that makes you like Spring,
So what is the magic this time of year brings?
It's the stalk! It's the stalk!

Festival-goers line up and file into the gazebo to sample each food entry in the rhubarb tasting contest and vote for the ones they consider the very best.

The farmer's market hums with vendors busily selling rhubarb salsa, rhubarb preserves, rhubarb nachos, rhubarb cookies, rhubarb lollipops, rhubarb bars, rhubarb bread, rhubarb roll-ups, fresh rhubarb and vibrant rhubarb plants. Amid all the food, one creative vendor offered homemade rhubarb soap.

A steady stream of tasters and voters choose from dozens of entries.

As eager taste-testers stand in line, budding athletes test their mettle in the Rhubarb Olympic games. The Rhubarb Stalk Throw determines who can throw a stalk of rhubarb the longest distance. To win at Rhubarb Golf a stalk is used to drive a ping-pong ball to a flag and the closest ball gets the prize. Rhubarb Hoops requires contestants to toss rhubarb stalks, free-throw style, into basketball hoops that are sized for small or tall players. One of the most challenging events is Green Eggs and Rhubarb. The goal is to successfully balance an organic green egg on a rhubarb stalk while walking around an obstacle course.

Rhubarb Stalk Throw:
throw a stalk of rhubarb
the longest distance.

Rhubarb Golf:
use a stalk to drive a ping
pong ball closest to a flag.

Rhubarb Hoops:
make a free throw with a
stalk.

Rhubarb Toss:
throw stalks into the holes
of a wooden beanbag
catcher.

Green Eggs and Rhubarb:
balance an organic green
egg on a stalk and walk
around an oobstacle
course without dropping
the egg.

19

Town celebrities pose in front of the gazebo after completing the Olympic Torch Run. The event started at Oz, a garden patch about a mile out of town. Runners passed the torch along the bike trail. It ended with transferring the flame at Sylvan Park.

Picnic tables are great spots to visit old friends and make new ones while enjoying a splendid array of rhubarb baked goods with a cup of rhubarb coffee. People meander through the park and read the cards attached to each apron that tells the story of who made it and why. Musicians and entertainers fill the air with rhubarb songs and individuals step up on a platform to present rhubarb rants. The Lanesboro Art Center table is overflowing with artistic supplies for children to make original Rhub-Art.

Creative vendors sell artistic rhubarb leaf birdbaths, earrings made from rhubarb leaves, rhubarb leaf vases and rhubarb leaf hats.

Throughout the day there is always a line for the "Ray and Ruby with their little Rhubarbettes" rhubarb photograph opportunity. Young and old look through four holes cut in a large colorful painting of rhubarb stalks. Joan Finnegan, an accomplished artist based in Lanesboro, painted the rhubarb and her husband, Wayne, cut the openings.

22

The daunting task of determining the largest rhubarb leaf and the heaviest rhubarb stalk is the responsibility of two carefully selected volunteer judges. They weigh, measure, tabulate and ultimately determine who has grown the largest leaf and which one weighs the most.

Norma Koch of Lanesboro has won largest leaf competition five years in a row.

Her largest leaf measured 41 inches wide and 49 inches long. It weighed 1.97 pounds.

23

At the end of the day anticipation mounts as the votes for the "best of the best" rhubarb tasting entries are tabulated by the bank clerk. The rhubarb cooks who have generously baked and served practically the entire town gather around the gazebo to find out who wins the prizes and takes home the highest respect.

Aprons are folded, clotheslines are taken down, the stage is picked up, and tablecloths and tables are put away as plans for the next year's festival are being made. All in celebration of rhubarb - the once lowly perennial that is rising up out of obscurity and receiving the attention it deserves.

The real gift of this festival and this book is in the knowing that down home, friendly places still exist, and in the reminder that the act of sharing food and fun can strengthen a community. Remember the Rhubarb Festival takes place on the first Saturday of June and you are invited!

Festival Roots

The idea for a rhubarb festival began in the spring of 2005 at a "44 Club" gathering (8 ladies, all born in 1944). Over dinner, ideas were tossed around on how to enliven our local farmer's market. This brainstorming led to Nancy Martinson and Mary Bell meeting with the Farmer's Market Board at the Lanesboro Pastry Shoppe. It was only a matter of a couple of days and the first rhubarb festival was scheduled for June 4, 2005 in Sylvan Park. The city administrator liked the idea, the Chamber of Commerce was all for it and the energy started to build.

Right from the get-go our vision for a rhubarb festival was to elevate the status of rhubarb and create a fun-filled celebration reminiscent of an old-fashioned get together where kids and adults play, eat, enjoy music and welcome everyone to participate. Our intention was to make our festival a "hoot."

Heidi Dybing jumped on board offering to make banners with her husband Phil bringing a sound system. Bonnie Handmacher readily accepted the challenge of orchestrating our own "Rhubarb Olympics." Peggy Hanson and Frank Wright liked the idea of a "Rhubarb Rant" and they recycled a wooden laundry box for festival participants to have the opportunity to pontificate about rhubarb.

We all agreed that the taste testing of rhubarb recipes had to be the highlight of the festival and the gazebo in the

25

center of Sylvan Park would serve as the perfect platform. To celebrate rhubarb, all festival participants would have the chance to taste each entry and vote for their favorites.

With a total budget of $600.00 we bought ads in local newspapers, printed brochures and invited everybody to bring enough rhubarb food to share. We encouraged people to enter their rhubarb in the largest leaf and heaviest stalk contests and to exercise their creativity with rhubarb art. Be it known--never underestimate the power of word-of-mouth in a small town!

As Minnesotans, we are aware that Garrison Keillor sings "Beboparebop Rhubarb Pie" on his Prairie Home Companion Radio Show, so we decided to try to get permission to use it as our theme song. Nancy Martinson drafted a letter (and as long as she was at it, invited him to our rhubarb festival.) We understood that the chance of him actually coming to our festival was slim (it was), but we were thrilled when he gave us permission to use his music.

Just a few weeks before our first festival we found out that Garrison Keillor was going to broadcast his radio show from nearby Rochester, Minnesota. This was an opportunity we could not pass up. The brainstorming took hold again and Heidi Dybing agreed to make red and green bibs with each bib displaying one letter that would ultimately spell rhubarb on the front and on the back. We needed at least 7 cohorts to pull

To pull this off we needed sponsors. Many businesses were glad to help - all donating money and prizes.

off this promotional gig. The rhubarb enthusiasts practiced the rhubarb song and then we all headed for the Prairie Home Companion. In the lobby prior to the show, we huddled in a circle, donned our bibs, got the letters straight so that we were spelling out r.h.u.b.a.r.b!! on both front and back and sang the rhubarb song over and over again. It didn't take long for one of Garrison's Duct Tape Squad staff to approach us to make sure we were not going to make a scene during the show. We gave him our festival brochure and then kept our fingers crossed in hopes that Garrison would mention our festival on the air. He did! In fact he mentioned it several times - and we were pumped.

We wanted to get the word out about our festival and our funny stunt worked!

As it turned out Heidi made 9 bibs to accommodate everyone who wanted to participate.

Once we had that Rhubarb song down, we decided to take the show on the road - not too far down the road, just about five miles to Whalen. This town is so small that they have a Stand Still Parade. There is only one street, no more than a block long, so the parade stands still and the people pass by. It is great fun! We once again sang our rhubarb hearts out while spelling "Rhubarb" and passing out information on our upcoming Rhubarb Festival.

Garrison Keillor Comes to Town

Our plotting, planning and scheming has led us from one thing to another. One morning in early March of 2007, while drinking coffee after yoga Nancy Martinson, our self-appointed top stalk of the Divine Rhubarb Committee, agreed to draft a letter to invite Garrison to our Rhubarb Festival. Lo and behold, the next thing we knew Garrison's people contacted the Lanesboro Chamber of Commerce and within a few days it was decided that "The Prairie Home Companion Show" would be broadcast from our baseball field during the 2007 Rhubarb Festival. The town went wild. "More Jell-O," cried Peggy Hanson, followed by, "we'll need more ham buns and calico beans."

March 12, 2007

Dear Garrison Keillor,

Lanesboro's third annual Rhubarb Festival will be Saturday, June 2, 2007. When you were in town for the Democratic fundraiser last September, the Rhubarb Sisters sang for the opening of your talk. You told them that there might be a possibility of being on your show in the future.

Well, those Rhubarb Sisters have been singing their little rhubarb hearts out just in case there might be an opportunity. How could we persuade you (or whoever needs to do that) to let them audition for a show? We, of course, are looking to promote our Rhubarb Festival on June 2.

Even though this festival is small in comparison to big city events, we believe that we are the only Rhubarb Festival that has a juggler who juggles flaming rhubarb, and we have Rhubarb Olympics for the whole family that includes not only tossing stalks, but carrying an organic green egg on a rhubarb stalk around an obstacle course. Now if that isn't down-home Minnesota fun, I just don't know what is! Plus we have food to sample from savories like Rhubarb Chili and salsas to sweets that are so yummy and drinks to top it off.

We offer this special invitation to you and your family to join in the fun. Just to be one of the real lovers of rhubarb in a town that believes food should be celebrated.

Very sincerely,
Nancy Martinson
The top stalk of the Divine Rhubarb Committee

The whole town was excited to see the stage go up with the Rhubarb banners!

We were surprised when it was decided that not only would Prairie Home Companion be broadcast on Saturday night, but they were planning another show for Friday night.

The week of the festival the stage for the show was set up in the Lanesboro softball field alongside the Root River. From there it was all hands on deck.

Fire trucks were moved out of the firehall to provide seating for the food events organized to feed visitors. Downtown business turned their roof outline lights on to dress up their buildings. For a small town having about 2,000 guests meant parking issues, shuttle services, food, signage, tickets, security, traffic control, lodging, fencing, sanitation and the help of lots and lots of volunteers. Electricity to the softball field and back-up generators proved to offer a series of interesting challenges. Because one of the main roads into town runs directly behind the softball field Garrison's crew asked if the highway could be closed during the performance. The producers did not want traffic noise in the background, especially truck drivers applying their brakes to traverse down the hill. Approval was given by the City Council to shut the highway down for two hours during the performances. This was a major happening.

On Friday night, just before the performance, the rain came and so did about 2,000 people in raincoats and carrying umbrellas. Because it was a BYOLC, "bring your own lawn chair" or picnic blanket event, people came carrying their seating accommodations.

When Garrison walked on stage the rain stopped and the crowd went wild. We roared and clapped and the fun began.

Garrison pointed to the two churches, one Catholic and the other Lutheran perched on top of the hill overlooking the town and the waterfall. He compared Lanesboro to his mythical town of Lake Wobegon.

Garrison sang with the Rhubarb Sisters and 16-year-old Yvonne Freese, toe tapped with Bob Bove and Gail Heil, danced with Orval and Marie Amdahl who were celebrating 65 years of marriage, and told story after story of life in Lanesboro. Then he launched into a woeful tale and offered rhubarb as a stress reliever and antidote for the problem by saying,

"Wouldn't this be a good time for a slice of rhubarb pie?" Again the audience roared. "Nothing gets the taste of shame and humiliation out of your mouth like Beboparebop Rhubarb Pie." Garrison made us all proud. It was a time like no other.

The next day was the Rhubarb Festival and Garrison came early and stayed late. He tasted everything rhubarb, shook hands with just about everyone and took in the festivities.

All day Saturday the weather was perfect. On the evening of the second performance the crowd was in place and Garrison was on stage. Then the rain came. It poured. There was a power outage. In the drenching downpour Garrison left the stage and walked out into the audience. He gave heart and soul to the crowd and the show went on with great style and panache.

More than 589 public radio stations nationwide with a weekly audience topping 4.3 million listeners heard Garrison express fondness for rhubarb and Lanesboro. In addition, the Armed Forces Network Europe, the Far East Network and dozens of European cities via the Astra satellite network heard Garrison sing our praises. It was thrilling to have this opportunity and the Lanesboro community has been continually grateful for this incredible gift.

On top of all this good fortune and fun, Peter Rosen, a new York film producer, followed Garrison to town to film footage for his Keillor documentary, "The Man on the Radio in the Red Shoes." The following year the people of Lanesboro were invited to a premier showing of Rosen's documentary at our St. Mane Theatre. The film includes many scenes of our town and the Rhubarb Festival. Lanesboro rolled out the red carpet for the premier.

The little girl handing Garrison flowers was unrehearsed. It was one of many magical moments of the day. Scene from Peter Rosen's documentary

37

Let's talk rhubarb

It is not red celery!

A rhubarb is defined as a heated dispute or a controversy.

Nancy Huisenga's

Nurse Nancy's Rant

Well, everyone, I'm here to talk to you about the thing that is nearest and dearest to your heart. . .
Rheum rhabarbarum L.,
Rhubarb - a garden vegetable

I know you're all wondering if it is a fruit or a vegetable. Rhubarb is actually a vegetable, often used as a fruit. It is a member of the buckwheat family.

Here are some little known (and probably little talked about) facts:
Rhubarb is native to China where historical records date it back to about 2700 B.C. Marco Polo brought it to fame in the West as a medicinal plant. For a period of time in the late 1700's through early 1800's, as a result of political conflicts, Chinese emperors forbade its export to the west.

Rhubarb has many uses and next to being a food, medicinal is the most common. For centuries rhubarb has been used in medicines and folk healing for centuries as a strong laxative and for its astringent effect on the mucus membranes of the mouth and nasal cavity.

Rhubarb exercises a digestive action and carries bile salts from the liver which stimulates the liver. Rhubarb performs by giving the taste buds a pleasantly bitter flavor that cleanses the oral cavity and prepares it to taste the coming food. When it reaches the stomach rhubarb's digestive effects come into full play, causing an increase of the flow of stomach juices and stimulating stomach digestive action and absorption. Besides stimulating the secretions from the liver, which carry the bile salts, it assists the intestine in regulating the absorption of fat.

40

Rhubarb leaves contain the poisonous substance oxalic acid which is corrosive and toxic to the kidneys. This acid is also present in spinach, cabbage, beet greens, and to some degree in potatoes and peas. The average lethal dose of rhubarb leaves would require a person to consume a rather unlikely eleven pounds of extremely sour leaves. In the stalks, the amount of the culprit oxalic acid is much lower but still enough to cause slightly rough teeth.

The roots and stems are rich in substances that are cathartic and serve as a laxative. This explains the sporadic abuse of rhubarb as a slimming agent. Chemicals naturally found in rhubarb are yellow or orange and can color the urine.

Rhubarb is 95% water. It is a good source of potassium, minor amounts of vitamins, and is low in sodium. Rhubarb's crisp sour stalks are rich in vitamin C, dietary fiber and calcium.

Ancient Chinese preparations mainly used the rhubarb rhizomes and roots. The strictly medicinal preparations are not recommended for old people, or those who suffer from heart diseases, kidney illnesses and pregnant women. Rhubarb should be avoided by those who suffer from oxalic gall stones, kidney stones, hemorrhoids and gout.

Claims have been made that it can inhibit cancer cells, treat worms and cure tired blood. As an aphrodisiac, rhubarb has been recommended for men and less for women. Next to ginseng, cinnamon and vanilla, rhubarb is one of Western Europe's famous aphrodisiacs.

Rhubarb is very low in sugar, making it an ideal low carbohydrate food except when you add the sugar and strawberries and pie crust!

10 Reasons to Plant Rhubarb

1. It's sweet-tart flavor is like none other.

2. It is the main ingredient in many comfort foods - pies, cakes and sauces - that conjure up nostalgic memories of mothers, aunts and grandparents.

3. You'll have enough to hand over the fence to your neighbors.

4. It is relatively pest and disease free and does not require toxic chemical inputs.

5. Deer, rabbits and woodchucks ignore it.

6. It grows with little attention in both good and poor soils.

7. It's one of the first vegetables of spring.

8. It comes back year after year.

9. It's been underutilized and undervalued. It is an "underdog." Everyone loves an underdog.

10. It's a way to "find happiness in your own backyard."

Growing Rhubarb

Rhubarb is a cool weather perennial that needs a period of cold dormancy to thrive. Mid-morning temperatures for two or more months that reach near or below freezing are required for rhubarb to die back, rest and prepare for the next spring. Southeastern Minnesota has many months of freezing temperatures and as a result we produce some of the best-rested rhubarb in North America. Most North American rhubarb production is in northerly states and Southern Canada.

Rhubarb will continue to produce succulent stalks as long as the monthly average temperature does not exceed 75 degrees. Higher temperatures cause the stalks to become tough and are no longer palatable.

For those who do not live in higher temperate latitudes or high elevation, you may be able to grow rhubarb as an annual by planting it in the fall, letting it over-winter and harvesting stalks the following season. To grow rhubarb in warmer climates you can try to keep the plants and soil cool. Sometimes the north side of a house, garage or shed can provide protection from blazing heat and help the rhubarb grow.

In the spring of 2010, Michelle Obama led school children in a dance and sang "Grow, rhubarb, grow," as they planted rhubarb in the White House garden - another example of light-hearted fun inspired by rhubarb.

A Rhubarb Couple

Frank Wright and his wife Peggy Hanson are known as "a rhubarb couple." Frank is a rhubarb aficionado, retired veterinarian, wood spoon artist and has well over 100 robust rhubarb plants. Peggy is a great cook, food blogger, Rhubarb Sister and philosopher when it comes to rhubarb.

Peggy believes, "Rhubarb stands for finding happiness in your own backyard. It is still popular in small towns and rural areas where lots of people have gardens and cook from scratch. Rhubarb evokes a simpler and less commercial existence - where the most important things are family, friends, perseverence, hard work and making do with what you have.

Frank says:
Personally, I've always thought a rhubarb survey should be part of the US census. With one question, "how many rhubarb plants are being maintained by this domicile?" we could learn so much about our selves and our communities.

Rhubarb is kind of old-fashioned, in a good way. And so is Lanesboro."

"The need for rhubarb is so great that soon it is going to be a target for thieves," Frank warns, "I'm advising people to put security lights on their rhubarb patch."

When spring arrives Frank and Peggy walk the streets and alleys of Lanesboro to note the number and vitality of rhubarb plants and scout out the healthiest and most robust. Frank says, "The only acceptable reason for a rhubarb index of zero is that it will not grow in your climate which is something you need to know before you invest in planting rhubarb."

"Most of my rhubarb comes from two patches planted between 25 and 80 years ago in Lanesboro," Frank boasts. "Who started them and what varieties they are nobody knows! They are robust, with thick stalks. One is a little redder than green and the other a little more green than red. They taste the same and if they didn't, it wouldn't matter because I mix all the stalks together to process."

Native to Siberia, the first written record of rhubarb is from 4,000 years ago. It came to Britain in the 13th century and was at that time more expensive than opium because it was considered a medicine. Rhubarb first came to the United States in the 1700s.

Planting Rhubarb

Rhubarb can be started from seeds but it takes a lot longer for it to produce than planting an established rhubarb crown. Greenhouses generally have robust rhubarb plants available.

Prospective rhubarb growers might consider scouting their neighborhood to find an attractive rhubarb plant. An established rhubarb plant can generally spare a cutting with no noticeable setback. Spring planting is preferred to provide assurance that the rhubarb receives enough rainfall to enable the taproot to become well established. With a shovel angled straight up and down, slice a slab off one side of the crown. The slab should have a couple of buds or stalks poking out of the top and roots coming on the bottom. Large, dense crowns can yield many divisions.

To plant, dig a hole at least one foot deep. Mix in rotted manure, peat moss, compost or other organic matter, such as manure tea. Organic matter hastens growth and helps the plant produce earlier. Research reports that rhubarb's best friend is horse manure. Yearly, in early spring or late fall top-dress the plant with additional organic matter. One pound of high nitrogen fertilizer will provide an abundant supply of food for one rhubarb plant.

Plant hills 3 to 4 feet apart. Hills should be divided and reset every 7 to 8 years or the plants become too thick and produce slender stalks.

One Farmer's Market vendor sells packages of sun-dried horse manure called, "Rhubarb's Best Friend," to strengthen under-fertilized and struggling rhubarb plants so they may reach their true potential.

Rhubarb does not like water to pool around the crown, causing it to rot.

The root of the plant is also referred to as the crown.

Harvesting Rhubarb

Rhubarb is one of the first vegetables to appear each growing season. You can almost watch it grow. At first a pinkish knob pushes through the earth and then baby leaves eventually unfold. Within a week the stalks can be six inches tall.

When seedpods and flowers appear, pull them from the base of the plant and discard. If the pods are left the energy of the plant goes into seed production instead of stalk growth.

Frank says:

Always pull the stalk -- never cut it!

Select firm, thick stalks. Reach down to the base of the stalk, sometimes it takes both hands, then pull the stalk up. I generally pull 1/3 to ½ of the plant at one time and over the course of the growing season I harvest 2 to 3 times. That means I do not take too much at one time, but ultimately take it all.

It is agenerally accepted practice to not harvest rhubarb the first year it is planted. However, I have found that if I have planted a sturdy crown I can pull a couple of stalks when they appear to be ready. I believe it stimulates plant growth. My experience with 125 rhubarb plants is pulling just a few stalks over the course of the first year is not harmful.

Leaf uses:
Use rhubarb leaves to cover vegetation you want to eliminate.
Leaves can be used to tan animal hides.
Rub rhubarb leaves over burnt areas on pots and pans to restore shine.
Rhubarb is an environmentally correct product that can be an effective organic insecticide for leaf-eating insects – cabbage caterpillars, aphids, peach and cherry slugs and more.

The root/crown of the rhubab polant can be used to make a fairly strong hair dye.

47

Commercial Production

In the United States commercial rhubarb production clusters are found in Washington, Oregon, California, Michigan and Ontario, Canada. Total commercial rhubarb production is estimated at less than 2000 acres. Home and farmstead rhubarb patches may well surpass the commercial crop.

Rhubarb production is on the rise because of the increased demand for locally grown produce and a widespread interest in rhubarb. Rhubarb is an attractive crop for urban agriculture and an exciting area of growth in food production.

These rhubarb plants at Featherstone Farm, in Rushford, Minnesota, were started from cuttings from Franks's garden. Frank's plants came from Stephanie Waldo's plants that were in her backyard in Lanesboro when she bought her house.

Frank's "Rhubarb News"

Frank uses a Comprehensive As-It-Happens Rhubarb Google alert system to keep his finger on the world's rhubarb pulse. Anytime the term "rhubarb" shows up in a news item, blog post, scientific abstract or an addition to a website, a link is sent to his email by the web crawlers.

He has found that rhubarb has become a darling of upscale restaurants and various food blogs. "Rhubarb sauces, chutneys and gastriques have become de rigueur over the past decade. Small wineries and farmer's markets are good consumers of local rhubarb. Community Supported Agriculture (CSA) farms are including rhubarb in their vegetable boxes."

Rhubarb grown in a hot house can have a lighter color and more delicate flavor.

Rhubarb grows prolifically in Siberia and in the Himalayas.

If you are using rhubarb as a landscaping or border plant the seed pods can add interest and height to a garden and do not need to be removed.

The Washington Rhubarb Growers Association reports that 2/3 cup of rhubarb has only 21 calories and supplies 24% of a person's daily calcium and 9% of vitamin C requirements.

Sweet Rhubarb Recipes

Rhubarb Jam

Adeline Deden

6 cups fresh rhubarb, cut in ½-inch pieces
4 cups sugar
One 21-ounce can apricot pie filling
One 2-ounce package lemon gelatin dessert

Pour sugar over rhubarb. Cover. Let sit overnight.
This causes juice to accumulate. Pour rhubarb
and sugar mixture into a large saucepan. Boil 10
minutes. Add apricot pie filling, return to a boil
and add lemon gelatin. Stir constantly until gelatin
has completely dissolved. Remove from heat,
pour into jars and seal.

Makes 4 pints

Rhubarb Rose Jam

6 cups fresh rhubarb, cut in 1-inch pieces
Water to cover rhubarb
3 cups organic rose petals, white heels removed
5 tablespoons fresh lemon juice
2½ cups sugar per pint of extracted liquid

Place rhubarb and 2 cups of petals in a medium saucepan. Add enough water to cover and cook over medium heat until tender. Add lemon juice.

Strain fruit through muslin or two layers of cheesecloth. Do not squeeze. Measure liquid. Add remaining rose petals and 2½ cups sugar for each pint of liquid.

Return to the saucepan and boil 10 minutes or until mixture reaches 220 degrees. Pour into jars. Process and seal.

Variations:

Rhubarb Rosemary Jam - Replace rose petals with a handful of rosemary leaves.

Rhubarb Wine and Roses Jam - replace rhubarb, water and lemon juice with rhubarb wine. Decrease sugar to 1¾ cups per pint of liquid.

Makes 2-3 pints

Raspberry Rhubarb Jam

5 cups fresh rhubarb, cut in ¼-inch pieces
3 cups sugar
One 10-ounce package frozen raspberries
9 tablespoons raspberry gelatin mix

Place rhubarb, sugar and raspberries in a large saucepan. Cook on medium heat for 20 minutes. Add gelatin mix for color.

Makes 2-3 pints

Lynn says this freezes well.

Breakfast is great with rhubarb jam on bread and butter but rhubarb chutneys, jams and conserves can also be served on scrambled eggs or souffles, in fruit compote or popovers.

The very same condiments accompany roasted and grilled meats very well and can turn these simple meals into works of art. As a glaze rhubarb conserves are worth their weight in gold on grilled ribs, salmon, shrimp, chicken, pork, lamb, vegetables and fruits.

12 cups fresh rhubarb, cut in ½-inch pieces
4 cups sugar
One 15-ounce can crushed pineapple
Two 3-ounce packages strawberry Jell-O®

Combine rhubarb, sugar, and pineapple in a large pan. Place over low heat and stir until sugar dissolves. Increase heat to medium and cook until mixture becomes clear and begins to thicken. Add Jell-O and stir to dissolve. Seal in sterilized jars, or cool and freeze in jars.

Makes 3-4 pints

This recipe uses more fruit and less sugar than most jam recipes.

1 medium orange
1 medium lemon
2 whole cloves
½ cup water
¼ cup distilled vinegar
1½ cups fresh rhubarb, cut in 1-inch lengths
3 cups sugar

Cut orange and lemon into very thin slices, remove
the seeds, and cut slices in half. Put slices in
a heavy enameled or stainless steel pan. Add
cloves and cover with water and vinegar. Simmer,
uncovered, for 15 minutes or until fruit is tender.

Add rhubarb and sugar and slowly bring to a
boil, mixing well. Reduce heat and simmer very
slowly, uncovered, stirring occasionally, until
thick. This may take up to 45 minutes. Remove
cloves. Refrigerate, unsealed, for three weeks.

Makes 2-3 cups

Rhubarb Conserve Adeline Deden

1 orange
6 cups fresh rhubarb, cut in 1-inch pieces
5 cups sugar
1/3 cup walnuts, coarsely chopped

Remove seeds from orange. Place entire orange, including skin, in food processor and grind.
Place all ingredients in a large pan. Boil and stir constantly for 15 minutes or until mixture becomes thick. Place in jars.

Makes 5-6 cups

Rhubarb jams, conserves and chutneys belong in the cheese course as well. Serve your rhubarb conserves and chutneys with strong cheese like gorgonzola or stilton on whole-grain bread or serve them with a mellow brie, cream cheese or herbed cheese spread on baked crisp toasts. Sharp cheddar and rhubarb taste great together and could be served on apple slices or dried pears. There are countless variations on this classic theme.

Blue Ribbon Blueberry Rhubarb Breakfast Sauce

Kirsten Ruen

6 cups fresh rhubarb, cut in ½-inch pieces
4 cups sugar
One 21-ounce can blueberry pie filling
One 3-ounce box raspberry Jell-O®

Place rhubarb and sugar in a medium saucepan. Boil 10 minutes. Add pie filling. Bring to a boil. Remove from heat and stir in Jell-O.®

Makes 4-5 cups

Tastes great on waffles, pancakes, muffins or toast.

Kirsten received a blue ribbon on her 4-H food preservation project at the Fillmore County Fair with this recipe.

Kirsten received a blue ribbon on her 4-H food preservation project at the Fillmore County Fair with this recipe.

Rhubarb Elderberry Syrup

2 cups elderberry juice, unsweetened
1 cup rhubarb juice, unsweetened*
2½ tablespoons fresh lemon juice
1¾ cups sugar or to taste
4 tablespoons cornstarch

Place elderberry juice, rhubarb juice and lemon juice in a medium sauce pan. Bring to a boil. Add sugar and cornstarch. Boil until thickened.

Makes 3 cups

Lynn says these recipes are Cottage House Inn favorites. This syrup is great served with pancakes, waffles or french toast.

*See page 142 for rhubarb juice recipe

Rhubarb Fluff Syrup for Waffles, Crepes or Pancakes

Barb Eickhoff

6 cups fresh rhubarb, cut in 1-inch pieces
1 cup water
13 ounces Marshmallow Crème

Place rhubarb in large pan. Add water. Cook over medium heat for 40 minutes, stirring occasionally, until there is no standing liquid and there are minimum fibers. Measure 1 cup of hot rhubarb sauce and place in a medium bowl. Add marshmallow crème. Fold together. Store in refrigerator.

This fluff syrup can be served chilled or heated in the microwave. (Watch it in the microwave – it may puff up.)

Makes 2 ½ cups

No need for sugar in this recipe. The marshmallow crème provides the sweetness.

Leftover unsweetened sauce may be stored in the freezer. Thaw, heat and make a batch of the fluff syrup when desired.

Chef's Choice # 3
Lynne's Rhubarb Bread

Lynne Jacobson

1/3 cup sugar
1 teaspoon cinnamon, ground
2 ½ cups flour
1½ cups fresh rhubarb, cut in ½-inch pieces
1 cup buttermilk
¾ cup white sugar
¾ cup brown sugar
½ cup oil
1 egg
2 teaspoons vanilla
1 teaspoon baking soda
1 teaspoon baking powder
1 teaspoon salt
¼ teaspoon nutmeg, ground

Mix 1/3 cup sugar and cinnamon in a small bowl. Set aside. Mix all remaining ingredients in a large bowl. Pour into greased 9-inch bread pan.

Top with sugar and cinnamon mixture. Bake at 350 degrees for 30-35 minutes.

Makes 1 loaf

Rhubarb Sweet Bread Gary Engstrom

2 cups all purpose flour or substitute half with whole wheat flour
1 ½ teaspoon cinnamon, ground
1 teaspoon baking soda
1 teaspoon fine sea salt
1 teaspoon ginger, ground
¼ teaspoon baking powder
1/3 cup fresh rhubarb juice*
1 cup sugar
½ cup brown sugar, packed
2 large eggs
1 cup rhubarb mash*
1/3 cup milk
½ teaspoon vanilla
½ cup walnuts, coarsely chopped
1/3 cup raisins

In a medium bowl, whisk together flour, cinnamon, baking soda, salt, ginger and baking powder, and set aside. Cream together rhubarb juice, sugar and brown sugar in a large mixer bowl. Beat in eggs, one at a time. Add rhubarb mash and beat on low speed until just blended. Mix milk and vanilla and add in three parts alternately with flour mixture. Beat on low speed until smooth, scraping the sides as necessary. Fold in walnuts and raisins.

Pour batter into a greased, 9 x 5-inch loaf pan and spread evenly. Bake at 350 degrees for 1 hour or until toothpick inserted into the center comes out clean. Cool pan on a rack for 10 minutes before unmolding. Unmold and allow bread to cool completely on rack.

Makes 1 loaf

See page 142 for Rhubarb Juice and Rhubarb Mash recipes

Rhubarb Muffins

¼ cup brown sugar
1 tablespoon butter, melted
1 teaspoon cinnamon
1 cup brown sugar
½ cup butter, softened
½ cup sugar
1 egg
2 cups flour
1 teaspoon baking powder
½ teaspoon baking soda
1/8 teaspoon salt
1 cup sour cream
3 cups fresh rhubarb
½ cup pecans, chopped

Variations: Substitute 1 cup strawberry yogurt for sour cream or ½ cup oatmeal for pecans.

In a small bowl, mix brown sugar, butter and cinnamon until crumbly. Set aside. In a large mixing bowl, cream sugar and butter. Add flour, baking powder, baking soda and salt. Mix. Add sour cream. Mix just until blended. Fold in rhubarb. Fill paper-lined muffin tins ¼ full. Sprinkle brown sugar mixture on top. Top with pecans. Bake at 350 degrees for 22 minutes or until toothpick inserted in centers comes out clean. Cool 5 minutes before removing from tins.

Makes 18 muffins

Rhubarb Crunch Muffins

For muffins:
2 ½ cups flour
1 ½ cups brown sugar
1 teaspoon cinnamon
1 teaspoon baking powder
1 teaspoon salt
1 egg
1 cup buttermilk
2/3 cup vegetable oil
1 teaspoon vanilla
2 cups fresh rhubarb, cut in ½-inch pieces

For topping:
½ cup sugar
1 tablespoon butter, melted
1 teaspoon cinnamon

Add a little oatmeal

In a large bowl, combine flour, sugar, cinnamon, baking powder and salt. In a small bowl, beat egg slightly. Add buttermilk, oil and vanilla. Mix together. Add egg mixture to dry ingredients. Add rhubarb. Combine only until moistened. Do not over mix. In a small bowl, mix together sugar, butter and cinnamon for topping.

Divide rhubarb batter evenly among greased or paper-lined muffin tins. Sprinkle topping over muffins. Bake in preheated 350 degree oven 20 minutes or until tops of muffins are light golden brown.

Makes 24 medium or 12 jumbo muffins

64

Rhubarb Love
by Steve Harris

I was a city kid from California visiting my grandparents'
Utah farm when I first discovered rhubarb. I was probably
around 13 or so. I remember a hot, dusty day, taking a walk
with a sweet girl with the prettiest blonde hair who lived
up the canyon. She surprised me when she reached down to
what I thought was a weed patch on the side of the dirt road
and broke off some greenish-red stalks. She started chewing
it, asked me if I wanted some, and wanting to be agreeable to
just about anything she might suggest, said, "sure."

A big bite later my mouth was filled with the sourest-tasting
stuff, kind of like killer celery. I didn't want to look dumb, so
I chewed it up, even took a second bite. Anything for a girl, I
guess. The walk ended, not sure if I ever saw her again, but
the memory of that first taste of rhubarb, in all its sour glory,
remains with me to this day.

Later I learned that with enough sugar, and fresh
strawberries from Grandma's garden, that same godawful
rhubarb could make quite a pie. There's a lesson about
transformation and redemption in there somewhere.

Susie says she thinks of Steve's Rhubarb Love story when
she's standing in her kitchen getting breakfast for her guests
and Steve goes out to pick fresh rhubarb. "But now I am the
girl in the story and HE makes the best rhubarb muffins ever!
Maybe these should be called Rhubarb 'Crush' Muffins!

I have strawberry rhubarb at the lake house, Mom has
Canadian rhubarb and I have a very nice patch of rhubarb at
Anna V's. Yes, I mix my rhubarb and proud of it!"

Steve remembers:
My dear Grandma, a God-fearing, three-time-a-week
church-going Grandma, gathered rhubarb each summer to
make what she called "rhubarb juice." The juice needed
to sit in the farmhouse cellar for a number of weeks before
it was "ready." It had quite a kick to it, as I remember. My
suspicions about the liquid were confirmed one Sunday
morning in church when she took my King James Bible and
pointed to Proverbs 20:1 ("Wine is a mocker and strong
drink is raging and whosoever is deceived thereby is not
wise.") With the pew pencil, and a little grin on her face, she
wrote the word "juice" in the margin.

Rhubarb Cobbler

Heidi Dybing

4 cups rhubarb
2 cups unbleached flour
¾ cups sugar
2 tablespoons flaxseed, ground
2 teaspoons baking powder
½ teaspoon salt
½ teaspoon nutmeg
¼ cup canola oil
2 cups apple juice

Place rhubarb in a 9 x 13-inch pan. Mix dry ingredients in a medium bowl. Add canola oil and mix with a fork until crumbly. Sprinkle mixture over rhubarb. Boil apple juice in a small pan and pour over dry ingredients until entire top is moistened. Bake at 350 degrees for 55 minutes or until crust is golden brown.

Makes 15 servings

Rhubarb Crunch

Doris Dybing

5 cups fresh rhubarb, cut in ½-inch pieces
1 cup sugar
4 tablespoons flour
1 cup brown sugar
1 cup oats
1 ½ cups flour
¾ cup butter
Optional: ice cream or whipped cream

In a large bowl mix first three ingredients and place in a 9 x 13-inch pan. For topping, use a fork to cut butter into sugar, oats and flour until it becomes crumbly. Sprinkle over filling. Bake at 375 degrees for 40 minutes.

Serve warm with ice cream or whipped cream.

Makes 15 servings

66

Chef's Choice Rhubarb Bars   Good!

Lynne Jacobson

2 cups flour
1 cup butter, softened
10 tablespoons powdered sugar
3 cups fresh rhubarb, diced
2 eggs, slightly beaten
1 ½ cups sugar
¾ teaspoon baking powder
½ teaspoon nutmeg, ground
¼ cup flour
¼ teaspoon salt

Mix first three ingredients in a medium bowl and pat into 9 x 13- inch pan. Bake crust for 10 to 12 minutes in a preheated 350 degree oven. Mix remaining ingredients for topping in a large bowl. Pour topping on crust and bake for an additional 35 minutes.

Makes 15 servings

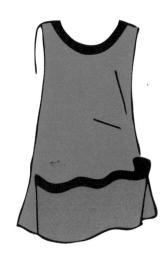

Rhubarb Bars

Lois Berekvam

3 ½ cups fresh rhubarb, cut in ½-inch pieces
2 tablespoons cornstarch
1 ½ cups sugar
1 teaspoon vanilla
1½ cups flour
1½ cups oatmeal
1 cup brown sugar
1 cup margarine
½ cup nuts, chopped
1 teaspoon baking soda

Simmer rhubarb, cornstarch and sugar in a medium saucepan, stirring constantly, until thick. Add vanilla and cool slightly. Set aside. Mix remaining ingredients in a medium bowl. Pour ¾ of oatmeal mixture in a 9 x 13-inch pan and pat down. Cover with cooked rhubarb filling. Top with the remaining crumb mixture.

Bake at 350 degrees for 35 minutes or until brown.

Makes 15 servings

Rhubarb Dream Bars

Mary Zika

2 cups all purpose flour
1 cup butter, softened
2/3 cup confectioners sugar
4 eggs, beaten
2 cups sugar
½ cup all purpose flour
1½ teaspoons salt
4 ½ cups fresh rhubarb, cut in ½-pieces
Cooking spray

In a medium bowl, mix flour, butter and confectioners sugar until a dough forms. Spray sides of a 9 x 13-inch pan with cooking spray. Press dough into bottom of pan. Bake at 350 degrees for ten minutes. While crust bakes, whisk together eggs, sugar, flour and salt in a large bowl. Stir in rhubarb to coat.

Spread evenly over baked crust when crust comes out of oven. Bake for an additional 35 to 45 minutes until rhubarb is tender. Cool and cut into squares.

Makes 15 servings

69

1 cup flour
½ cup butter
5 tablespoons powdered sugar
2 eggs
1½ cups sugar
¼ cup flour
¾ teaspoons baking powder
2 cups fresh rhubarb, cut in ½-inch pieces
½ teaspoon salt

Mix flour, powdered sugar and butter until crumbly. Pat into bottom of an 8-inch square pan. Bake at 350 for 15 minutes or until brown. Beat eggs until fluffy. In a separate bowl, mix together sugar, flour and baking powder and gradually add to eggs.

Add rhubarb and mix together. Mix in salt. Pour over crust. Bake at 350 for 35 minutes. The egg mixture comes to the top and forms a meringue.

Makes 9 servings

Lena's Rhubarb Tart

Cheryl Jordahl
Cheryl Abelmann

1 cup sifted flour
½ cup butter
2 tablespoons sugar
Dash of salt
3 cups fresh rhubarb
1¼ cups sugar
3 egg yolks
½ cup cream
2 heaping tablespoons flour
Dash of salt

Topping:
Top with powdered sugar and strawberries

Alternate Topping:
In a small bowl, mix 3 egg whites, stiffly beaten,
together with 6 tablespoons sugar
and ¼ teaspoons cream of tartar.

Pour over baked rhubarb mixture. Brown in oven.

Blend flour, butter, sugar, and salt in a medium bowl until crumbly. Pat into a 9 x 9-inch pan and bake at 350 degrees for 30 minutes. Combine remaining ingredients in a medium saucepan. Cook until mixture thickens and rhubarb is tender. Pour over baked crumb crust. Bake at 350 for 45 minutes.

Top with either of the topping options.

Makes 9 servings

Rhubarb Coffee Cake

Yvonne Nyenhuis

1½ cup brown sugar, packed
½ cup shortening
1 egg
2 cups flour
1 teaspoon soda
½ teaspoon salt
1 cup sour cream
1½ cups fresh rhubarb, cut in ½-inch pieces
½ cup chopped pecans
¼ cup sugar
¼ cup packed brown sugar
1 tablespoon butter or margarine
1 teaspoon cinnamon, ground
Optional: Substitute walnuts for pecans

Cream sugar and shortening in a medium mixing bowl. Add egg and mix well. In a separate bowl, combine flour, soda and salt.

Add dry ingredients and sour cream alternately to sugar and shortening mixture. Fold in rhubarb. Pour into a greased 9 x 13- inch pan. Combine remaining five ingredients with a fork in a medium bowl. Sprinkle on top. Bake 45 to 50 minutes in a preheated 350 degree oven.

Makes 15 servings

Yvonne found this recipe in Anna Belle's Kitchen in the Fillmore County Journal.

First Place
Rhubarb Cake

8 cups fresh rhubarb, cut in ½-inch pieces
4 cups apple, cut in ½-inch pieces
5 cups all-purpose flour
2 teaspoons baking soda
4 teaspoons salt
1 cup butter
3 cups sugar
2 eggs, beaten
2 teaspoons vanilla
2 cups buttermilk
2 cups brown sugar
1 cup pecans, chopped
1 cup butter, softened
2 cups sugar
1 cup evaporated milk

In a large bowl stir together rhubarb and apples.
Pour into two 9 x 13-inch pans. Set aside.

In a small bowl mix together flour, soda and salt.
Set aside. Cream together butter, sugar, eggs and
vanilla. Add flour mixture to butter and sugar
mixture, alternating with buttermilk. Pour over
fruit in pans. Sprinkle brown sugar and pecans
on top. Bake at 350 degrees for 1 hour. Cream
together butter and sugar. Add evaporated milk
and mix well. Pour on top of cake while cake is
still hot.

Makes 30 servings

73

Second Place
Rhubarb Custard Cake

Pat Heath

One 18.5-ounce box yellow cake mix plus
ingredients listed on package
6 cups fresh rhubarb, cut in ½-inch pieces
1 cup sugar
2¾ cups whipping cream, not whipped

Lightly grease 9 x13-inch pan. Prepare cake batter
according to package directions. Pour batter into
pan. Spread rhubarb evenly over batter. Sprinkle
sugar on rhubarb. Pour whipping cream over
everything. Bake 1 hour at 350 degrees. Flip cake
over to serve.

Makes 15 servings

Rhubarb Birdsnest

Doris Schuck

3 cups fresh rhubarb, diced
¾ cup sugar
2 cups flour
½ teaspoon salt
½ cup shortening
½ cup sour milk
2 eggs
1 teaspoon vanilla
¼ cup sugar

Place rhubarb in a medium bowl. Add ¾ cup
sugar and mix. Set aside. In a large bowl stir
together flour and salt. Add shortening, sour
milk, eggs and vanilla to flour mixture. Beat until
smooth. Spread rhubarb in a 9 x 9-inch pan. Pour
batter over top. Sprinkle with sugar and bake at
350 degrees for 45-50 minutes. Serve warm.

Makes 9 servings

Rhubarb Delight

Dona Conway

2 cups unbleached flour
2 teaspoons baking soda
1 teaspoon cinnamon, ground
½ teaspoon allspice, ground
½ teaspoon salt
½ cup butter
1 cup honey
2 eggs, beaten
½ cup plain yogurt
1 teaspoon vanilla
3 cups fresh rhubarb, cut in ½-inch pieces
½ cup walnuts, chopped

Mix flour, baking soda, cinnamon, allspice and salt in a medium bowl. Set aside. In a separate bowl, cream together butter, honey, eggs, yogurt and vanilla. Combine dry with wet ingredients. Add rhubarb and walnuts.

Place in a greased 9 x 13-inch pan and bake at 350 degrees for 30 to 35 minutes.

Makes 15 servings

75

Rhubarb Cake

Margaret Lukkason

3 cups fresh rhubarb, cut in ½-inch pieces
2½ cups miniature marshmallows
1¾ cups sugar
2 eggs
1¾ cup flour
3 teaspoons baking powder
½ cup milk

Mix rhubarb, marshmallows and ¾ cup sugar
and pour into a 9 x 13-inch pan. Beat eggs and
remaining sugar until thick and lemon colored.
Add flour and baking powder. Mix in milk. Pour
over rhubarb. Bake at 350 degrees for 45 minutes.

Makes 15 servings

5 cups fresh rhubarb
One 3-ounce package strawberry Jell-O®
1 cup sugar
3 cups miniature marshmallows
One 18.5-ounce box yellow cake mix plus
ingredients listed on package
1 cup heavy whipping cream
1 tablespoon sugar
½ teaspoon vanilla

Lightly grease a 9x13-inch pan. Layer rhubarb, Jell-O, sugar and marshmallows in pan. In a large bowl, prepare cake mix according to package directions. Pour prepared cake batter over rhubarb. Bake 1 hour at 350 degrees. Cool in pan 1 hour. Place whipping cream in a chilled medium glass or metal bowl. Beat with an electric mixer until soft peaks form. Add sugar and vanilla.

Beat until stiff peaks form. To serve, turn cake upside down and top with whipped cream.

Makes 15 servings

Cream Cheese and Mascarpone Cheesecake with Stewed Rhubarb

Rhubarb Sister
Robin Scheu

For crust:
6 ounces unsalted butter, softened
½ cup plus 2 tablespoons sugar
1 ¼ cups all purpose flour
1 ¼ cups yellow cornmeal
½ teaspoon salt
Cooking spray

For cheesecake:
1 ½ pounds cream cheese, softened
1 ¼ cups sugar
½ pound mascarpone cheese, slightly softened
Zest of 1 orange and 1 lemon
5 eggs plus 1 egg yolk
¼ cup heavy cream
1 tablespoon vanilla extract
¼ teaspoon lemon extract

For Stewed Rhubarb and Raspberries:

2 ½ cups fresh rhubarb, cut in ¼-inch pieces
2/3 cup sugar, plus more to taste
¼ cup orange juice
2 tablespoons water
1 pint fresh raspberries

In mixer fitted with paddle, cream butter and sugar until light and fluffy. In small bowl combine flour, cornmeal, and salt. Add to butter mixture. Mix until well combined. Spray bottom and sides of a spring form pan with cooking spray. Press mixture evenly onto the bottom and sides of pan. Chill crust 15 minutes to set. Place in preheated 350 degree oven. Bake until lightly golden. Remove pan from oven. Cool. Wrap bottom with foil to seal. Reduce oven to 325°F.

In mixer fitted with paddle, beat cream cheese,

78

sugar and mascarpone on low speed until smooth. Add zests. Add eggs and yolk, one at a time. Beat on low speed until smooth and well combined. Add cream and extracts. Mix until just combined. Pour mixture into cooled shell. Place pan in a larger baking pan. Fill larger pan with hot water to reach half way up sides. Bake until set but still wobbly in center, 65-70 minutes. Remove cheesecake from oven. Let cool in waterbath. When completely cool, remove from waterbath. Chill at least 2 hours or overnight.

In a saucepan, place rhubarb, sugar, juice and water over medium heat. Simmer gently, stirring occasionally, until sugar is dissolved and rhubarb is almost tender. Using a slotted spoon, remove rhubarb from liquid. Transfer to a medium bowl, set aside. Raise heat to medium, and continue until thickened and reduced slightly. Remove from heat. Transfer reduced liquid to a small bowl to cool. Add the cooled, thickened liquid to the reserved cooked rhubarb. Stir to combine.

To serve, combine stewed rhubarb with raspberries. Spoon fruit over cheesecake and enjoy!

Makes 12 servings

Robin's sister, a chef at Cooks of Crocus Hill in the Twin Cities, recommends this rhubarb dessert.

Rhubarb Cheesecake

Char Johnson

1 cup flour
¾ cup oatmeal
½ cup butter
½ cup brown sugar
½ teaspoon cinnamon
8 ounces cream cheese, softened
¾ cup sugar
1 egg
½ teaspoon nutmeg, ground
¼ teaspoon cinnamon, ground
2 cups fresh rhubarb, cut in ½-inch pieces

Combine flour, oatmeal, butter, brown sugar and cinnamon in a medium bowl. Mix until crumbs form. Pat half of mixture in a 9 x 9-inch pan. In a small bowl, combine cream cheese, sugar, egg, nutmeg and cinnamon. Blend until smooth. Gently stir in rhubarb. Spread filling over crust. Top with reserved crumbs. Bake for 40 to 45 minutes at 350 degrees. Cool and keep refrigerated.

Makes 9 servings

Hershey® chocolate brownie base:
1 cup sugar
1 stick butter melted
4 eggs
One 16-ounce can Hershey® chocolate syrup
1 teaspoon vanilla
1 cup flour
½ teaspoon salt

Place all ingredients in a medium bowl and mix well. Fill greased mini-muffin cups 2/3 full and bake at 350 degrees for 10 to 12 minutes. Remove from oven and stamp round impression in center of each cup. Fill each impression with one tablespoon rhubarb sauce and then white chocolate ganache, and top with candied rhubarb slice.

White Chocolate Ganache:
8 ounces cream cheese

¼ cup powdered sugar
1 tablespoon milk
2 ounces white chocolate (heat in microwave for 30 seconds or until melted)
1 ½ cup Cool Whip®
Mix cream cheese, sugar, milk and chocolate in a small bowl. Fold in Cool Whip®.

Rhubarb Sauce:
4 cups rhubarb, cut in ½-inch pieces
¾ cup sugar
2 tablespoons water
3 tablespoons minute tapioca
Place in small saucepan and cook over medium heat until rhubarb is tender.

Candied Rhubarb:
1 cup rhubarb, sliced
1 tablespoon water
Coat with sugar, steam for three minutes

81

Strawberry-Rhubarb Pizza

Inn at Sacred Clay Farm
Sandy Kiel

Pizza Dough:
1½ cups flour
2 teaspoons baking powder
½ teaspoon salt
6 tablespoons cold butter cut into cubes
½ cup plus 2 tablespoons cold milk

Sauce:
6 medium rhubarb stalks, cut in ½-inch pieces
¾ cup sugar
¼ cup Marsala® wine

Topping:
1 cup water
¾ cup sugar
1 cup fresh rhubarb slices, bias-cut in ½-inch pieces
1 cup fresh strawberries, sliced

½ teaspoon nutmeg, freshly grated
2 tablespoons butter, melted
2 tablespoons Grand Marnier

Dough: Mix flour, baking powder and salt in food processor. Add butter and pulse 30-35 times or until dough forms pea-size pieces. Add cold milk and pulse just until combined. There will be small clumps. Turn out onto a floured surface. Knead a few times and push or poke the dough into a 12-inch circle. Place on a greased cookie sheet. Raise the edge slightly to hold in the sauce and topping.

Sauce: Place rhubarb pieces, sugar and Marsala wine in a medium saucepan. Gently cook over medium heat 10 minutes or until rhubarb is very soft, stirring occasionally. Let cool slightly while preparing topping.

Topping: Place water and sugar in a small saucepan. Bring to a boil. Add rhubarb slices and nutmeg . Return to a boil. Remove from heat. Add sliced strawberries and immediately strain liquid from fruit. Set fruit aside. Bring liquid to a boil again and reduce to 1/3 cup.

Assemble: Spread sauce over pizza dough. Top with sliced strawberries and rhubarb topping, leaving an edge that's uncovered. Drizzle melted butter and Grand Marnier over top. Bake in a preheated 450 degree oven for 20 minutes or until crust is golden. Remove from oven and pour reduced syrup over top. Let cool for 10 minutes.

Makes 8 servings

Sandy suggests serving with a scoop of sorbet or fresh fruit slices. Feel free to be creative!

Strawberry-Rhubarb Rustic Galette

For sweet galette dough:
¾ cup unbleached all-purpose flour
¼ cup cornmeal
1 teaspoon sugar
½ teaspoon salt
7 tablespoons unsalted butter, chilled, diced into small cubes
3 tablespoons sour cream
1/3 cup ice water

For filling:
1 large egg
1 teaspoon heavy cream
1/3 cup hazelnuts, toasted, husked and chopped
¾ cup plus 1 tablespoon sugar
3½ cups fresh rhubarb, trimmed, cut in 1/3-inch thick slices

10 ounces fresh strawberries, hulled, thickly sliced
3 tablespoons cornstarch
2 tablespoons strawberry preserves
½ teaspoon ground cinnamon

Sift flour, cornmeal, sugar and salt together in large bowl. Cut in butter to resemble bread crumbs. Add ice water and sour cream. Mix until combined. Form into disc. Wrap in plastic. Chill until firm.

Preheat oven to 400 °F. Place 9-inch diameter tart pan bottom on parchment- lined baking sheet. Roll out dough on floured work surface to 13-inch round. Transfer to prepared baking sheet, centering over tart pan bottom.

For filling:

Beat egg with cream to make a glaze. Brush dough with 1/3 of glaze. Sprinkle hazelnuts over dough. Mix ¾ cup sugar and next 5 ingredients in a large bowl. Mound rhubarb mixture in center of dough, leaving 1½-inch border. Fold dough border over filling, pleating loosely and pinching any cracks to seal. Brush crust with remaining egg glaze. Sprinkle crust with 1 tablespoon sugar. Bake tart until crust is brown and filling bubbles, about 55 minutes. Transfer baking sheet to rack and cool.

Makes 6 servings

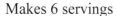

Robin's sister, a chef at Cooks of Crocus Hill in the Twin Cities, recommends this dessert.

Rhubarb-Strawberry Pie

Filling:
2 cups fresh rhubarb, cut in ¼-inch pieces
2 cups fresh strawberries, sliced
1¼ cups sugar
¼ cup minute tapioca
1 tablespoon butter
Prepared pie crust
Variation: Add 1 teaspoon orange zest to filling

Mix all ingredients in a medium bowl. Let stand
15 minutes. Line 9-inch pie plate with pie crust.
Fill with fruit mixture. Dot with butter. Cover
with top pie crust. Seal and flute edge. Cut
several slits in top crust. Bake in preheated 400
degree oven for 45-50 minutes or until juices form
bubbles that burst slowly. Cool.

Makes 8 servings

Bea's Rhubarb Pie

Beatrice Burmeister

Filling:
1 ¼ cups sugar
1 egg
¼ cup Half and Half
2 tablespoons flour
Dash of salt
3 cups fresh rhubarb, cut in ½-inch pieces

Double Crust:
2/3 cup Crisco®
2 cups flour
1 teaspoon salt
3 tablespoons ice water

For Filling:
In a medium bowl, mix sugar, egg, half and half, flour and salt for filling. Add rhubarb and set aside.

For Crust:
In a separate bowl, cut Crisco into flour and salt using a pastry blender or two table knives. When mixture resembles coarse crumbs, add ice water, a little at a time, with a fork until crumbs hold together. With your hands gently form dough into two separate balls. With a rolling pin, roll out each ball on a floured surface to form two 12-inch circles for top and bottom crusts. Place bottom crust in pan, add filling, put on top crust. Use a sharp knife to make several cuts through top crust to allow steam to escape. Bake at 400 degrees for 10 minutes. Reduce heat to 350 degrees and bake an additional 40 minutes.

Makes 1 pie

When using frozen rhubarb, do not thaw.

Chef's Choice #2
Classic Rhubarb Pie

Loni Kemp

Basic Piecrust*
Makes three crusts

3 cups flour
1 cup butter, unsalted, cut into chunks
1 tablespoon sugar
1 teaspoon salt
1 egg
6 tablespoons cold water

Place flour, butter, sugar and salt into a food processor and process up to ten pulses until mixture resembles coarse meal. Beat egg in a cup with a fork and add water. While processing, gradually pour liquid into processor, mixing 30 seconds at most. Divide dough into three parts, wrap each in wax paper and chill one hour, or freeze ten minutes. Keep extra crust in freezer for another use.

*from Food from an American Family Farm: three Generations of Family Recipe Secrets by Janeen (Schrock) Sarlin, 1991, recalling her girlhood on a Fillmore County dairy farm.

Filling
5 cups fresh rhubarb, sliced (can be fed through tube of food processor)
1¼ cup sugar
¼ cup minute tapioca
2 teaspoons orange zest, finely grated

88

Combine filling ingredients and let sit for 15 minutes to bring out juices. Meanwhile, roll out one crust and drape over rolling pin to lay into a 10-inch pie pan. Add the filling. Roll out second crust and cut into 1-inch wide lengths, and weave a lattice top on the pie. Crimp edges. Sprinkle crust with sugar if desired.

Bake at 350 degrees in convection oven for 45-50 minutes (or at 450 degrees for 10 min then at 350 degrees for 35-40 minutes in regular oven.) Juices will bubble slowly when the pie is done. Cool.

Makes 1 pie

Rhubarb Pie

Evelyn Marzolf

3 cups fresh rhubarb, cut in ½-inch pieces
2 eggs, beaten
1 ½ cups sugar
3 tablespoons flour
1 tablespoon butter, melted
¼ teaspoon nutmeg, ground
1 unbaked pie shell

In a medium bowl mix eggs, sugar, flour, butter and nutmeg and pour over rhubarb. Mix well. Pour into unbaked pie shell. Bake at 375 degrees for 10 minutes. Reduce heat to 350 degrees and bake an additional 45 minutes.

Makes 1 pie

Evelyn makes a lattice top to put on top of pie. Roll a prepared crust into a circle and cut into ¾-inch strips. Moisten the edge of the bottom crust. Lay two strips in an X pattern across the center of the pie. In an over-and-under fashion, weave remaining strips into a lattice pattern. Trim ends of each strip to the outer edge of the bottom crust and press edges together to seal.

Rhubarb-Maple Toasted Bread Pudding

Dr. Kay Johnson

4 slices white bread
¾ cup milk
3 tablespoons butter
2 eggs
¼ cup maple syrup
¼ cup plus 1 tablespoon sugar
1 pinch salt
1 cup fresh rhubarb, cut in ½-inch pieces

Topping:
1 cup heavy whipping cream
1 tablespoon sugar
Splash of maple syrup

Remove crusts from bread. Toast slices. Tear into small cubes and place in a medium bowl. Heat milk in a small saucepan with 2 tablespoons of the butter. Pour over bread cubes and let soak for one minute. Use remaining butter to coat a 1-quart casserole dish. In a medium bowl beat together eggs, maple syrup, ¼ cup sugar and salt. Stir in rhubarb. Combine with bread mixture. Pour into buttered casserole, sprinkle remaining sugar on top and bake for 40 minutes in a preheated 325 degree oven.

Topping:
Place whipping cream in a chilled medium glass or metal bowl. Beat with an egg beater or electric mixer until soft peaks form. Add sugar and a splash of maple syrup. Beat until stiff peaks form.

Serve pudding warm with topping.

Makes 4 servings

Dr. Kay says this recipe is best if made with a good quality white bread – "homestyle." bread

Candied Rhubarb

4 cups fresh rhubarb, cut in ½-inch slices
2 cups sugar
1 tablespoon water

In a medium saucepan, cook rhubarb with water until rhubarb is slightly soft. Drain and cool. Add sugar to coat rhubarb. Using dehydrating machine, dehydrate rhubarb until dry.

Makes 2 cups

Biscotti

½ cup slivered almonds
2 ½ cups all purpose flour
1 cup sugar
4 tablespoons butter, softened

1 tablespoon anise seeds
2 teaspoons baking powder
1 teaspoon vanilla
¼ teaspoon salt
3 large eggs
2 cups candied rhubarb
Optional: White chocolate coating

Preheat oven to 350 degrees. Place almonds in baking pan; toast in oven 10 minutes or until lightly browned, stirring occasionally. Cool and set aside.

Place 1½ cups of flour, sugar, butter, anise seeds, baking powder, vanilla, salt and eggs in a large bowl. With mixer on low speed, beat ingredients until just mixed; increase speed to medium and beat 3 minutes, occasionally scraping bowl. In a separate bowl, coat the rhubarb and almonds with some of the remaining 1 cup of flour. Stir rhubarb, almonds and remaining flour into the batter, mix until blended. Wrap dough with plastic wrap and refrigerate 1 hour or until firm enough to handle.

Grease 2 large cookie sheets. Divide dough in half. On well-floured surface, with floured hands, shape each half of the dough into a rope, approximately 15 inches by 2 inches. Place on cookie sheets. Bake at 350 degrees for 25 minutes or until lightly browned.

Remove cookie sheets from oven. With serrated knife, cut hot loaves crosswise in ¾ inch thick slices. Lay slices cut-side down on same cookie sheet, making sure they do not touch. Return to oven and bake cookies 5 minutes. Turn and bake 5 minutes more. Remove to a wire rack to cool. Makes 3 Dozen.

Rhubarb Pudding

3 cups rhubarb, diced
1¼ cups water
¾ cup brown sugar
¼ cup white sugar
3 tablespoons butter
3 tablespoons cornstarch

Place all ingredients in a microwave-safe bowl.
Mix and microwave on high for 8 minutes or until
thick.

Makes 2 cups

*Verna says this is good served either warm or
chilled.*

Chocolate Rhubarb Pudding

Nancy Martinson

6 cups fresh rhubarb, cut in 1-inch pieces
2 cups water
1 cup sugar
8 ounces semi-sweet chocolate chips

Combine rhubarb, water and sugar in a medium saucepan. Cook over medium high heat 10 to 15 minutes. Do not stir. Cook until rhubarb has softened, then stir and add chocolate chips. Continue to stir until chocolate has thoroughly melted. Serve at room temperature or chilled. Top with whipped cream or ice cream.

Makes 6 servings

Nancy says to make sure you do not stir the rhubarb mixture while it is cooking.

Serve with whipped cream or ice cream.

Rhubarb Fruit Soup

12 cups fresh rhubarb, cut in ½-inch pieces
3 quarts water
2 cups sugar
2½ cups raisins
1 8-ounce box Minute Tapioca®
1½ teaspoons cinnamon, ground

Place all ingredients in large saucepan. Bring to a
boil and simmer for 20 minutes or until rhubarb is
soft. Serve warm or cold.

Makes 12 servings

Lip Smacking Compote

8 cups fresh rhubarb, cut in 1-inch pieces
6 large Granny Smith apples, peeled and cut in
thin slices
1 quart strawberries, cut in half
1 cup sugar
½ cup apple juice
3 cinnamon sticks
1 tablespoon candied ginger, minced
2 teaspoons orange peel, grated
½ teaspoon nutmeg, ground

Combine all ingredients in a 5-quart slow cooker.
Cover and cook on low about 5 hours, or until
rhubarb softens.

Makes 10 cups

*Carol says this is great topped with whipped cream
and a sprinkling of nutmeg. Or use it as a topping
for ice cream.*

97

Delicate Poached Rhubarb with Ricotta

1/2 cup sugar
1/2 cup water
2 teaspoons fresh lemon juice
2 cups fresh rhubarb, cut in ¾-inch pieces
1 tablespoon rose-water

2 cups ricotta cheese
2 tablespoons cream
1 tablespoon sugar
1/2 teaspoon vanilla

Bring sugar, water and lemon juice to a boil in a medium sauce pan. Reduce heat and gently simmer until sugar dissolves. Add rhubarb and simmer for 3 minutes. Remove from heat and cover pan. Allow to cool for 5 minutes and stir in rosewater Return cover to pan and cool.

Combine ricotta, cream, sugar and vanilla in a medium bowl. Mix with electric mixer until smooth. Serve poached rhubarb in shallow bowls with scoops of ricotta.

In this recipe the poached rhubarb is sweetly scented & clear pink and its tartness contrasts nicely with the rich cheese.

Makes 4 servings

Rhubarb Yogurt

4 cups fresh rhubarb, cut in 1-inch pieces
1 cup sugar
1 cup water
½ teaspoon nutmeg, ground
2 cups plain yogurt

Combine rhubarb, sugar, water and nutmeg in a
medium saucepan. Simmer for 20 minutes until
sauce thickens. Cool in refrigerator. Just before
serving, add one part yogurt to one part rhubarb
sauce.

Makes 4 servings

Third Place
Rhubarb Fruit Fluff

Barb Eickhoff

3 cups fresh rhubarb, cut in ½-inch pieces
½ cup water
1 cup sugar
One 8-ounce package cream cheese
¾ cup sugar
One 8-ounce can crushed pineapple, drained
1 cup fresh or frozen strawberries
2 bananas, sliced
½ cup pecans, chopped
One 12-ounce tub Cool Whip®

Place rhubarb in a medium pan with water and 1 cup sugar. Cook down over medium heat until it becomes a sauce. Taste. If too tart add sugar. Cool the sauce.

Combine cream cheese with ¾ cup sugar. Add pineapple. Add cooled rhubarb sauce, strawberries, bananas and pecans. Fold in Cool Whip. Freeze in 9 x13 inch pan or individual cups.

Makes 15 servings

This is great as salad or dessert.

100

Rhubarb Ginger Hibiscus Freeze

Liz Belina

1 pound crystallized ginger
8 cups fresh rhubarb, cut in 1-inch pieces
1 cup water
One 3-ounce box red Jell-O®
1 cup strong sun-brewed hibiscus tea
1 cup local honey

Instead of using an ice cream freezer, pour mixture into a cake pan and place in freezer. Stir several times while freezing for a smoother consistency.

Makes 3 quarts

Finely mince ¼ of the crystallized ginger. Set aside. Bring rhubarb and water to a boil in a large pan. Cook for 5 minutes or until rhubarb is tender. Set aside ¼ of chunky pulp. While rhubarb is still very hot, add ¾ pound of crystallized ginger and Jell-O. Allow to soften 5 minutes. Puree. Add back in the chunky rhubarb pulp. Add the minced ginger, hiciscus tea and honey. Chill well. Freeze in ice cream freezer.

Liz says the hibiscus tea balances the rhubarb bitterness.

Serve as a pick-me-up on a hot afternoon. Or as a light, sweet-tart finish to any fine meal. Enjoy the bounty of healthful benefits from rhubarb, ginger, hibiscus and honey.

Rhubarb and Strawberry Sorbet with Mint

Inn at Sacred Clay Farm
Sandy Kiel

9 cups fresh rhubarb, cut in 1-inch pieces
2 cups sugar
2 teaspoons vanilla
2 pints strawberries, cut in quarters
4 tablespoons orange juice concentrate
2 tablespoons water
2 tablespoons fresh mint leaves

Combine rhubarb, sugar and vanilla in a large saucepan. Bring to a boil. Reduce heat and simmer for 20 minutes. Cool from boiling temperature to warm. Puree in food processor until smooth. Add strawberries, orange juice concentrate and water. Process until smooth. Add rhubarb mixture and process until well blended. Add fresh mint leaves. Process just until evenly distributed. Chill in the fridge until completely cool. Pour into ice cream maker. Process and freeze. Makes 1 quart.

Third Place
Rhubarb Ice Cream

Mary Bell

1 gallon vanilla ice cream
1 cup red rhubarb flakes*
1 cup raw rhubarb flakes*

Melt ice cream. Stir in rhubarb flakes.
Combine thoroughly, refreeze, then serve.

Makes 1 gallon

See page 144 for rhubarb flakes recipes.

Rhubarb Popcorn

Mary Bell

½ cup dried red rhubarb flakes*
2 tablespoons dried raw rhubarb flakes*
2 tablespoons butter
¼ cup corn syrup
1 teaspoon vinegar
12 cups popped popcorn

In a small bowl combine the rhubarb flakes together. In a saucepan, melt butter, then add corn syrup and stir. When blended add the dried rhubarb. Stir. Add vinegar. Over medium-high heat, bring to a boil and cook to the soft ball stage. Pour over popcorn and mix vigorously until popcorn is coated.

Makes 12 cups

*See page 144 for rhubarb flakes recipes

6 cups rhubarb juice*
4 cups orange or pineapple juice
4 cups 7-Up® or Sprite®
Sugar
Water

Combine first three ingredients. When serving,
add sugar and water to taste.

Makes 14 cups

*See page 142 for rhubarb juice recipe

Rhubarb Slush

Nancy Martinson

8 cups fresh rhubarb, diced
3 cups sugar
8 cups water
½ cup lemon juice
One 3-ounce package strawberry Jell-O®
7-Up® or Sprite®
Optional: vodka

Combine rhubarb, sugar, water and lemon juice in a large pan. Cook over medium heat approximately 15 minutes until mushy. With a strainer, drain, save juice and discard pulp. While still warm, add strawberry Jell-O to juice. Put into containers and store in freezer. To serve, scoop frozen mixture into glasses. Add 7-Up or Sprite to taste.

Makes 1 gallon of frozen mixture

Add vodka if desired.

Great drink for a party!

Habberstad House Strawberry Rhubarb Pomegranate Lemonade

Habberstad House
Nancy Huisenga

8 cups frozen rhubarb, cut in 1-inch pieces
Three 12-ounce packages frozen strawberries
3 cups sugar
3 cups water
3 tablespoons lemon zest
One 16-ounce bottle pomegranate blueberry juice
1½ cups lemon juice, fresh squeezed
Frozen lemonade concentrate to make 2 quarts
when mixed with water

In a large pan, cook rhubarb, strawberries, sugar,
water and lemon zest together. Boil until soft.
Cool and puree in blender. Add pomegranate
blueberry juice and lemon juice. Dilute with water
to taste. Chill thoroughly and serve. Garnish as
desired.

Makes 1 gallon

Savory Rhubarb Recipes

Rhubarb Garden Salsa

Jerilyn Eddy

24 medium tomatoes, chopped
5 cups rhubarb, chopped
5 hot peppers, chopped
2 bell peppers, chopped
2 minced garlic cloves
1 medium zucchini, chopped
1 small yellow squash, chopped
1 large onion, chopped
1 cucumber, chopped
1 cup corn
2 cups cider vinegar
½ cup lemon juice
½ cup sugar
¼ cup canning salt
Variation: Add more peppers if you like it hotter.

Mix all ingredients in a large pan and bring to boil. Reduce heat and simmer for 10 minutes. Chill and serve.

To preserve this salsa, pour in jars while still hot, cover, and place in a hot water bath for 30 minutes.

Makes 5 quarts

1 cup sugar
¼ cup water
1 tablespoon finely shredded orange peel
6 cups fresh rhubarb, sliced in ½ pieces
½ cup green bell pepper, diced
1/3 cup red onion, finely chopped
¼ cup sweet onion, finely chopped
1 jalapeno, washed and stemmed
2 tablespoons honey
2 tablespoons lemon juice
1 teaspoons grated fresh ginger
hot sauce to taste

In medium pan combine sugar, water and orange peel. Bring to boil over high heat. Add the rhubarb and reduce heat to medium. Simmer gently 20 minutes or until rhubarb is tender.

Remove from heat and cool to room temperature. Transfer to a food processor fitted with steel blade or blender and process until smooth. Scrape the puree into a large bowl and add bell pepper, sweet onion, red onion, jalapeno, honey, lemon juice and ginger. Mix well. Serve at room temperature or chilled if desired. Serve with chicken or turkey or as a topping over leafy greens.

Makes 4 cups

Glee says serve this salsa with chicken or turkey or as a topping over leafy greens

2 tablespoons grated horseradish
.85 ounce dry ground mustard (entire McCormick® short round container)
18 ounces apple jelly
18 ounces apricot preserves
One 5-ounce can crushed pineapple, well drained
7 cups fresh rhubarb, peeled and finely chopped

Combine horseradish and dry ground mustard in a large bowl. Add jelly, preserves and pineapple. Refrigerate this while you're preparing the rhubarb. Fold in rhubarb. Chill. Serve with chips or crackers of your choice.

Makes 8 cups

Barb says this salsa is not for the faint of heart. You may want to make half a recipe.

Rhubarb Chipotle Sauce

Jennifer Wood

10 cups fresh rhubarb, cut in 1-inch pieces
2 cups white sugar
½ cup brown sugar
¼ cup water
1 cup diced onion
1 tablespoon olive oil
2 cloves garlic, diced
¾ cup raspberry vinegar
¼ cup chipotle peppers in adobo sauce
1 teaspoon brown mustard
Dash of salt

In a large pan, cook rhubarb with sugars and water over medium heat, stirring often, until rhubarb is very soft and falls apart. Set aside. In a medium skillet, sauté onions in olive oil until very soft and slightly brown. Add garlic and continue cooking on medium heat for one minute.

Add onion/garlic mixture to rhubarb and boil gently for 5 minutes. Remove from heat. Add remaining ingredients. Stir well and cool. Place in blender and blend until smooth.

Makes 6 cups

Try serving over cream cheese as an appetizer or as a dip for pretzels. May be used as a salsa.

113

Rhubarb Gastrique

1 cup sugar
½ cup red wine vinegar
3 cups fresh rhubarb, cut in 1-inch pieces
Variation: White wine vinegar may be substituted for red wine vinegar.

Mix sugar and vinegar in a medium saucepan. Bring to a boil and cook stirring occasionally, until liquid is reduced by half, stirring occasionally. Add rhubarb and simmer 10 minutes. Strain rhubarb mixture using a sieve, pressing down on solids. Store in a glass jar in refrigerator. Serve as a condiment with grilled or broiled meats or with whatever strikes your fancy.

Makes ¾ cup

Peggy says gastrique is a thick syrup made with a sugar and vinegar or wine reduction and fruit or fruit preserves.   It is often used to add a savory fruit flavor to meat dishes. It can be made with blackberries or tangerines or plums or...rhubarb!

114

Rhubarb Mint Chutney

Dr. Kay Johnson

1 tablespoon butter
1 small onion, minced
3 cups fresh rhubarb, cut in 1-inch pieces
2/3 cup sugar
¼ cup lemon juice, fresh
1 teaspoon mint, chopped fine
½ teaspoon lemon zest, grated
Salt to taste
Pepper to taste

Melt butter in large skillet over medium heat.
Add onion and cook for 3 minutes or until soft.
Add rhubarb, sugar, lemon juice, mint and lemon
zest. Bring to a boil. Stir constantly until sugar
dissolves. Reduce heat and simmer, uncovered,
for 5 to 7 minutes or until thickened. Season with
salt and pepper.

Makes 1½ cups

*Dr. Kay says chutney can be prepared, cooled,
covered and refrigerated for up to 2 days. Serve
with lamb.*

115

Rhubarb and Onion Chutney
Elaine Hove

4 cups fresh rhubarb, cut in ½-inch pieces
4 cups brown sugar
2 cups white onion, chopped
2 cups vinegar
1 teaspoon cloves, ground
1 teaspoon allspice, ground
1 teaspoon cinnamon, ground
Optional: red pepper flakes

Combine all ingredients in a medium saucepan and boil slowly until thick. Seal in jars or freeze.

Add red pepper flakes if you like it hot.

Makes 6 cups

At lunch rhubarb chutney is particularly good used as is or mixed with mayonnaise as a sandwich condiment. Sliced meat, cheese and hearty breads are all perfect compliments. Serve it for dinner with toasted walnuts, roasted garlic, caramelized onions and goat cheese on salad greens or pizza. And for your next large gathering consider using rhubarb chutney as a dip for cold shrimp, breadsticks, flatbreads, onion rings and fried vegetables.

2 tablespoons butter
1 tablespoon olive oil
5 stalks of fresh rhubarb, cut in 1-inch pieces
1 cup sweet onion, chopped
1 tart apple, peeled and cut in1-inch pieces
1 cup fresh cranberries
½ cup sugar
1 teaspoon cloves, ground
1 teaspoon cumin, ground
1 teaspoon cinnamon, ground
½ teaspoon allspice, ground
Optional: ½ cup fresh or frozen raspberries
Variation: Substitute frozen cranberries or craisins for fresh cranberries.

Heat butter and olive oil in medium sauce pan. Add rhubarb, onion and apple. Cook over medium heat. Stir. Add cranberries, sugar and spices. Simmer for 10 minutes. You may need to add a little more butter or a few tablespoons of water.

After the chutney is cooked, gently fold in raspberries.

Makes 4 cups

Mimi serves this with pork loin, turkey or chicken.

Rhubarb Ketchup

Barb Eickhoff

4 cups fresh rhubarb, diced
4 cups fresh tomatoes, chopped
3 medium onions, chopped
1 cup white vinegar
1 cup brown sugar
1 cup white sugar
1 tablespoon pickling spice
2 teaspoons salt
1 teaspoon cinnamon, ground

Combine all ingredients in a large saucepan.
Simmer over medium heat until mixture is thick.

Makes 2 pints

Canned diced tomatoes plus tomato puree may be substituted for fresh chopped tomatoes.

Stores well in refrigerator or freezer.

Carter's Pickled Rhubarb D'lites

Carter Larson

12 cups rhubarb, cut in 1-inch pieces
1 cup vinegar
3 cups sugar
5 cups water
½ teaspoon cinnamon
One 14-ounce box of red hot cinnamon candy

Cut rhubarb and put into jars. Bring the rest of the
ingredients to a boil. Pour over rhubarb in the jars.
Let cool. Store in refrigerator.

Makes 6 pints

Beet Pickles

2 pounds beets
Water to cover beets
1 ½ cups sugar
1 cup Scenic Valley® rhubarb wine
¾ cup apple cider vinegar
8 to 10 Red Hot® candies

In a medium saucepan boil beets with water over medium heat until tender. Drain. Cool beets. Rub off skins. Slice large beets; leave small beets whole. Return beets to pan. Add sugar, wine, vinegar and red hots. Boil until beets are heated through. Place in clean glass jars. Refrigerate.

Makes 2 pints

The jars may be processed as pickles to store unrefrigerated.

Minty Rhubarb Cream Cheese

1 cup fresh rhubarb, cut in ½-inch pieces
¼ cup water
8 ounces Neufchatel cheese, softened
1½ teaspoons fresh mint, chopped fine
Variation: Substitute cream cheese for Neufchatel

In a small saucepan cook rhubarb in water until it
is the consistency of soupy applesauce. Pour into
a medium bowl. Add Neufchatel cheese and mint.
Cream until smooth.

Makes 1½ cups

*Beth suggests serving with bagels, crackers,
vegetables or pretzels.*

Minted Rhubarb Soup

Dr. Kay Johnson

1½ cups white grape juice
1/3 cup granulated sugar
¼ cup fresh mint leaves
6½ cups fresh rhubarb, cut in 1-inch pieces
1 pint fresh raspberries
½ cup mascarpone cheese
1 tablespoon powdered sugar
Optional: raspberries and mint leaves for garnish

Bring grape juice and granulated sugar to a gentle boil over moderate heat in a large, nonreactive saucepan. Stir until sugar dissolves. Remove from heat. Add mint leaves. Let stand 15 minutes. Remove mint. Return pan to moderate heat and bring juice to a boil. Add rhubarb and simmer until soft, about 10 minutes. Reduce heat to low. Add raspberries and simmer 5 minutes longer. Remove from heat. Cool. Puree mixture.

Strain through a sieve into a large bowl. Cover and chill for at least 2 hours. Whip the cheese and powdered sugar in a small bowl until thick. Serve soup in chilled bowls. Top with a dollop of whipped mascarpone.

Garnish with fresh raspberries and mint.

Makes 4 servings

Dr. Kay says that you may refrigerate leftovers and enjoy the next day.

Lentil-Rhubarb Soup

1 ½-cups boiling water
¾ cup lentils
4 cups water
2 tablespoons bouillon chicken basee
2 tablespoons olive oil
2 cups carrots, chopped
1 ¾ cups celery, chopped
1 ½ cups onion, chopped
1 cup fresh rhubarb, cut in ½-inch pieces
¼ cup parsley, divided
1 tablespoon tomato paste
½ teaspoon salt
¼ teaspoon black pepper
6 tablespoon sour cream

Variations: Vegetable base may be substituted for chicken bouillon. You may omit bouillon or omit using chicken stock in place of water.

Yogurt or crème fraiche may be substituted for sour cream.

Soak lentils in boiling water while you prepare the remaining ingredients. Mix 4 cups water with chicken base and whisk to combine. Heat a large pan over medium heat and add olive oil. Sauté carrots, celery and onion for 4 minutes or until slightly softened. Add rhubarb and half the parsley and continue sautéing for 2 minutes. Drain lentils and add to pan. Add tomato paste and salt. Bring mixture to a boil. Cover, reduce heat, and simmer 25 minutes or until lentils are tender.

Cool the soup slightly and serve with a sprinkling of parsley and a dollop of yogurt or sour cream.

Makes 6 servings

2 tablespoons vegetable oil
¾ cup onion, chopped
3 garlic cloves, minced
1 pound ground pork
1 pound ground beef
One 14 ½-ounce can beef broth
One 28-ounce can crushed tomatoes
2 tablespoons balsamic vinegar
1/3 cup raisins
2 tablespoons chili powder
½ teaspoon allspice, ground
¼ teaspoon cloves, ground
½ teaspoon salt
One 14-ounce can black beans
2 cups fresh rhubarb, diced
Optional: ¼ cup slivered almonds

Heat vegetable oil in a large Dutch oven. Stir in onion and garlic. Cook until soft. Add pork and beef. Cook until browned. Drain off excess fat. Add beef broth and tomatoes. Stir in vinegar, raisins, spices and salt. Bring to a boil. Reduce heat and cook 30 minutes, partially covered. Uncover and cook for another 30 minutes. Add black beans and rhubarb and cook an additional 10 minutes.

Serve chili with almonds sprinkled on individual servings if desired.

Makes 8 servings

Vicki suggests experimenting with different balsamic vinegars. She's tried black cherry balsamic which resulted in a slightly fruitier edge to the chili.

Dean's Rhubarb Chile

Dean Hove

1 ½ pounds ground beef
1 tablespoon olive oil
1 onion, chopped
1 cup sweet red pepper, chopped
1 cup sweet yellow pepper, chopped
½ cup Scenic Valley Rhubarb wine
2 cups fresh rhubarb, cut in 1-inch pieces
One 14.5-ounce can chopped tomatoes
One 14.5-ounce can diced tomatoes and green chilies
One 14.5-ounce can tomato sauce
½ cup ketchup
1 bay leaf
1 teaspoon chili powder
1teaspoon cayenne pepper, ground
1 teaspoon garlic powder
Optional: Add salt and pepper to taste

Brown hamburger with olive oil in a large pan. Add onions and sweet peppers to hamburger. Sauté until vegetables soften. Add rhubarb wine. Simmer over medium heat for 5 minutes. Add remaining ingredients and bring to a boil. Reduce heat to low and cook for 30 minutes. Serve.

Makes 8 servings

Rhubeans
Heidi Dybing

2 cups dry pinto beans
8 cups water
12 cups water
1½ cups fresh rhubarb, cut in ½-inch pieces
1 cup onion, chopped
¾ cup brown sugar
½ cup maple syrup
1½ teaspoons salt
½ teaspoon dry mustard
¼ teaspoon pepper
Variation: Use 4 cups canned pinto beans instead of dry beans

In a large pan, soak beans overnight in 8 cups water. Rinse. Add 12 cups water and simmer 45 minutes or until beans are soft. Drain beans and save liquid. Pour beans into roaster. Add remaining ingredients and stir together. Pour bean liquid over mixture to cover, adding additional water if necessary. Bake covered at 325 degrees for 2½ to 3 hours. Uncover and cook down to desired consistency.

Makes 6 to 8 servings

Make it for a crowd:
4 pounds dry pinto beans (equals 20 cups cooked)
Water to cover for soaking
Water to cover for cooking
8 cups fresh rhubarb, cut in ½-inch pieces
5 cups onion, chopped
3½ cup brown sugar
3 cups maple syrup
2 tablespoons salt
2½ teaspoons dry mustard
1½ teaspoons pepper

126

1 cup dried orange lentils
1 large sweet potato, peeled and sliced
1 tablespoon olive oil
1 cup fresh rhubarb, diced
2 tablespoons plus 1 teaspoon sugar
1 tablespoon curry powder
1 teaspoon ginger, freshly grated
1 teaspoon hot red chili powder
Optional: Substitute canola oil for olive oil
            Salt and pepper to taste
            Shredded coconut for garnish

Cover lentils with water in a deep pot. Bring to a boil. Reduce heat and add sweet potato slices. Simmer 45 minutes or until soft. Remove from heat and drain if necessary. Mash with a fork and set aside. Heat oil in a medium skillet until hot. Add rhubarb. Stir and cook until tender.

Stir in the remaining ingredients. Add to mashed lentils. Pour into a medium baking dish. Bake 20 minutes until hot.

Garnish with coconut if desired.

Makes 4 servings

Nancy says to serve this hot with cooked brown rice.

127

1 teaspoon mustard seeds
1 cup onion, chopped
1 tablespoon olive oil
2 teaspoons garlic, minced
2 teaspoons fresh ginger, grated
1 red chili pepper, minced
1 teaspoon cumin
½ teaspoon turmeric
4 cups beef broth
1 ¼ cups red lentils
1 ½ cups fresh rhubarb, cut in ½ -inch pieces
2 teaspoons sugar
1 teaspoon lemon juice
½ teaspoon salt
½ cup sweet red pepper, chopped
½ cup fresh parsley, chopped
Variations: ½ teaspoon dry red pepper flakes may be substituted for red chili pepper. Chicken broth,

vegetable broth or water may be substituted for beef broth. Add ½ cup chopped tomato with red pepper and parsley if desired.

Heat mustard seeds in a large, dry skillet until seeds pop. Add olive oil, garlic, ginger, chili pepper, cumin and turmeric. Cook one minute over medium heat until fragrant. Add broth and lentils. Cover and reduce heat. Simmer 20 minutes or until mixture is thick and creamy. Stir in red pepper and parsley.

Serve with pita pieces and parsley.

Makes 4 servings

Veg, Fruits and Beef with Israelis Couscous

Joan Finnegan

1 pound beef round steak , cut in 1-inch cubes
1 tablespoon olive oil
1 teaspoon cumin
½ teaspoon cinnamon
½ teaspoon salt
¼ teaspoon black pepper
2 cloves garlic, minced
2 large onions, chopped
1 cup water
2 tablespoons jalapeño peppers, chopped
2 bay leaves
4 sweet red peppers, cut in 1-inch pieces
1 cup fresh or frozen rhubarb, cut in ½-inch pieces
½ cup dried apricots, cut in ½
½ cup dried cherries
1/3 cup kalamata olives, pitted

In a large skillet, combine round steak, olive oil, cumin, cinnamon, salt and pepper. Brown lightly. Add garlic and onions. Continue cooking 10 minutes over medium heat. Add water, jalapeño peppers and bay leaves. Cover and slow simmer 2 hours or until meat is tender. Stir occasionally. Add more water if needed. Stir in red peppers, rhubarb, apricots, cherries, and olives. Cook over medium heat for 10 minutes.

Makes 4 servings

Joni says to serve with fresh parsley and fresh lemon slices over Israelis couscous. Brown rice will substitute nicely for the couscous.

2 pounds beef round steak, cut in 1-inch pieces
2 large onions, chopped
1 tablespoon olive oil
2 cups chicken stock
1 cup water
¼ cup lemon juice, freshly squeezed
¼ cup fresh parsley
2 teaspoons mint, dried
1 generous teaspoon saffron
1 teaspoon sea salt
1/2 teaspoon black pepper
3 cups fresh or frozen rhubarb, cut in ½-inch
pieces
Variation: Add more sea salt to taste

Brown round steak and onions with olive oil in a
large skillet. Sauté 10 minutes or until tender.

Add chicken stock, water, lemon juice, parsley,
mint, saffron, salt and pepper. Stir and cover.
Simmer on low heat 2 hours or until beef is tender.

Serve over cooked brown rice.

Makes 12 servings

Joan says:
*I found this Iranian recipe 15 years ago and kept
it because it intrigued me. I have adjusted and
tweaked the ingredients a little but overall it is the
same. The rhubarb is folded in the last 15 minutes
of cooking so the flavor does not take back stage.*

Rhubarb Pork Chop Hotdish

4 boneless pork loin chops
1 tablespoon canola oil
Salt and pepper to taste
2½ cups soft bread crumbs
3 cups fresh rhubarb, cut in 1-inch pieces
½ cup brown sugar, packed
¼ cup flour
1 teaspoon cinnamon, ground
Variation: Substitute frozen rhubarb for fresh.

In a large skillet, brown pork chops in oil.
Sprinkle with salt and pepper. Remove chops and
keep warm. Mix ¼ cup pan drippings with bread
crumbs. Reserve 1/2 cup coated crumbs. Sprinkle
remaining crumbs in a 9 x 13-inch pan, sprayed
with cooking oil. In a large bowl, combine
rhubarb, sugar, flour and cinnamon. Spoon half of
rhubarb mixture over bread crumbs in pan.

Arrange pork chops on top. Spoon remaining
rhubarb mixture over chops. Cover with foil
and bake at 350° for 30minutes. Remove foil.
Sprinkle with reserved bread crumbs. Bake
15 minutes longer or until a meat thermometer
reaches 160°.

Makes 4 servings

131

Barbeque Sauce for Sloppy Joes

Barb Eickhoff

Sauce:
3 cinnamon sticks
1 tablespoon whole cloves
1 teaspoon whole celery seed
1 cup white vinegar
14 cups fresh rhubarb, cut in 1-inch pieces
2 cups water
Six 6-ounce cans tomato paste
1 cup sugar
Optional: Add more sugar to taste

Break cinnamon sticks into pieces and place in a small saucepan. Add cloves and celery seed. Add vinegar and bring to a boil. Remove from heat. Let stand while preparing and cooking rhubarb.

Place rhubarb into a large, heavy pan. Add water and cook for 1 hour or until no chunks are left. Add tomato paste and sugar, stirring after each can of tomato paste is added. Simmer until hot. Pour vinegar mixture through a sieve and add to rhubarb. Discard spices. Cover and cook over low heat for 30 minutes. Sauce will sputter and splatter; leave the pan lid slightly ajar.

Makes 6 pints
1 pint of sauce is enough for 2 pounds of ground meat

Barb says make the spiced vinegar before you go to the garden to pick the rhubarb. This allows the vinegar to steep. Spices steep in vinegar just like tea. This separate brewing adds to the deep color of the sauce.

Sloppy Joes:
2 pounds ground pork
1 tablespoon dried minced onion
1 teaspoon salt
1 teaspoon Mrs. Dash®
2 cups sauce
*Variation: Substitute ground beef, ground chicken
or ground turkey for ground pork*

Sloppy Joes:
In a large skillet,brown meat with minced onion,
salt and Mrs. Dash. Add sauce to meat. Heat and
serve.

Kool Rhubarb and Strawberry Salad

Jacque Crutcher

4 cups fresh rhubarb, cut in one-inch pieces
1½ cups sugar
1 tablespoon strawberry Kool-Aid®
1 cup water
Three 3-ounce packages strawberry gelatin
2 cups boiling water
One 10-ounce package frozen strawberries
1 cup celery, diced
¾ cup walnuts, chopped

Combine rhubarb, sugar, soft drink powder and water in a medium saucepan. Bring to full rolling boil. Remove from heat. Cover and let stand until cool. In a large bowl, dissolve gelatin in boiling water. Add frozen strawberries. Stir until thawed. Fold in rhubarb mixture, celery and nuts. Pour into a 9 x 13 pan or large mold. Chill until set.

This may be poured into a large mold for a beautiful presentation.

Jacque likes to serve this salad on a bed of greens.

Makes 12 servings

134

Roasted Rhubarb Salad

3 cups fresh rhubarb, cut in ¾-inch pieces
¼ cup honey
½ cup walnut pieces
¼ cup canola oil
2 tablespoons sugar
2 tablespoons raspberry vinegar
1/2 teaspoon salt
1/8 teaspoon pepper
6 ounces mixed salad greens
½ cup feta cheese, crumbled

In a medium bowl, toss rhubarb with honey. Place on a rimmed cookie pan. Roast for 5 minutes in a 450 degree oven. Remove pan from oven. Cool rhubarb on pan for 30 minutes or until rhubarb is cool and softened. Place walnuts on a separate baking sheet. Roast at 450 degrees for 3 minutes. Remove from oven. Cool and chop.

In a small bowl, mix oil, sugar, vinegar, salt and pepper until thoroughly blended. Place greens in a large bowl. Mix with just enough dressing to coat greens. Add rhubarb and walnuts . Toss. Sprinkle feta cheese on top.

Makes 4 servings

135

Braised Red Cabbage and Rhubarb

2 tablespoons mustard seed
1 tablespoon fennel seed
2 tablespoon olive oil
1 medium onion, thinly slices
1 medium head red cabbage, cored & thinly sliced
1 cup fresh or frozen rhubarb
1 cup cider or red vinegar
1/3 cup honey
1 teaspoon orange zest
1 bay leaf
½ teaspoon salt
½ teaspoon pepper

Lightly toast the fennel and mustard seeds in a small sauté pan over medium heat. Grind the toasted spices in a spice/coffee grinder or with a mortar and pestle. Heat olive oil in a large pan over low heat and sauté onions 6 minutes or until soft. Add ground spices and continue cooking 5 minutes. Add remaining ingredients in order given, stirring after each addition. Cover and cook 15 minutes over medium heat. Uncover, reduce heat to low and cook for one hour. Stir occasionally. Add salt and pepper. Remove bay leaf before serving.

Makes 4-6 servings

Basic Rhubarb Recipes

This rhubarb recipe collection would not be complete without a recipe for basic rhubarb sauce. While we're at it we're including recipes for juice, mash and dried rhubarb. Rhubarb prepared in these ways knows no limits other than your imagination.

Basic Rhubarb Sauce

Heidi Dybing

2 cups fresh rhubarb, cut in 1-inch pieces
1 cup water
½ cup sugar

Simmer rhubarb, water and sugar in a small saucepan for 15 minutes or until rhubarb softens and sauce thickens.

Makes 2 cups

If you prefer a thicker sauce, use less water.

Visitors to Lanesboro are delighted to find that Lanesboro hospitality often includes home cooking featuring rhubarb sauce. It is quick, delicious and its tart sweetness compliments vanilla ice cream, pound cake, popovers, cornbread and thick slices of whole grain raisin bread. Rhubarb sauce is great added to yogurt and oatmeal and can be served on everything from pancakes and waffles to pork chops.

One pound of rhubarb, cut in ½-inch pieces equals 4 cups.

Rhubarb stalk strings can be peeled off, but it isn't necessary.

A small amount of beet juice may be added to sauce, juice or mash for color.

What Shall We Do With the Extra Rhubarb?

What shall we do with the extra rhubarb,
What shall we do with the extra rhubarb,
What shall we do with the extra rhubarb,
Earlye in the morning?

Hooray, how well it freezes,
Hooray, how well it freezes,
Hooray, how well it freezes,
Earlye in the morning!

Bake it in a crisp with the extra berries,
Slice it in a salad and top with dressing,
Simmer it with beans and you've got chili,
Earlye in the morning!

Chorus

Boil it with vinegar and can some pickles,
Dry it in the sun for rhubarb leather,
Mash it in a blender and make a smoothie,
Earlye in the morning!

Chorus

That's what we'll do with the extra rhubarb,
That's what we'll do with the extra rhubarb,
That's what we'll do with the extra rhubarb,
Earlye in the morning.

A parody of The Drunken Sailor, a traditional sea shanty. New lyrics by Beth Hennessy as sung by The Rhubarb Sisters.

4 cups frozen rhubarb
1 cup water

Place a colander in a medium bowl. Place frozen rhubarb in the colander. As rhubarb thaws, juice will drain into the bowl. When the rhubarb is completely thawed, press the pulp using a large spoon or rubber spatula to extract additional juice. Pour juice into a storage container and set aside.

Place rhubarb pulp in a medium saucepan. Add water and simmer until pulp falls apart. Return colander to the bowl and allow the excess juice to drain off the mash. This bonus juice can be either added to the juice collected, or discarded.

Makes 1 1/2 - 2 cups juice and 1/2 cup mash.

Use fresh rhubarb juice as a substitute in recipes for vinegar or lemon juice.

Use rhubarb mash as a substitute for pumpkin puree (or other similar ingredients) when making breads, cakes, sweet breads or muffins.

Lanesboro's cooks never like to see rhubarb go to waste. Juicing rhubarb is a great way to use the season's bounty. Juiced rhubarb can be used fresh or frozen for use later. Rhubarb juice tastes great mixed with lemon, strawberry, orange, pineapple, ginger, mint or vanilla.   Add sparkling water, soda water or ice teas. Sweeten to taste with sugar or honey to make an endless array of healthy flavorful drinks.

Mashing is one of the quickest way to utilize large amounts of rhubarb. Fresh or frozen rhubarb mash can add flavor, texture and nutrition to many different recipes. Mash is an excellent substitute for apple sauce, pumpkin puree and fats in baked good such as breads and muffins and it is a tasty addition to soups, stews and chili.

Rhubarb freezes well. Juice, mash or cut-up fresh rhubarb may simply be put in a storage container and placed in the freezer. It's that easy.

Rhubarb may also be canned. Check with canning guides for canning instructions.

To dry rhubarb you will need a food dehydrator that has solid plastic liner sheets, called "leather" sheets.

Raw rhubarb flakes

2 cups fresh rhubarb, cut in 1-inch pieces
2 cups boiling water

Place rhubarb in a stainless steel pot and cover with boiling water. Let sit at least 1 hour, until rhubarb changes color. Blanching helps eliminate some of the acidity and softens the texture so it's easier to puree. Drain off water and place rhubarb in small batches in a blender to avoid overtaxing the blender.

Lightly oil leather sheet with cooking oil to prevent the mixture from sticking. Pour rhubarb puree evenly over leather sheet. Place leather sheet in a drying tray and dry at 135 degrees until rhubarb is hard. Place dried rhubarb in a bowl and crush with your hands to make flakes.

Red rhubarb flakes

3 cups rhubarb
3 cups boiling water
2 tablespoons strawberry gelatin

Place rhubarb in a stainless steel pot and cover with boiling water. Let sit at least 1 hour, until rhubarb changes color.

Drain off water and place rhubarb in small batches in a blender. Add gelatin and blend again. Lightly oil the leather sheet with cooking oil to prevent mixture from sticking. Pour rhubarb puree evenly over leather sheet. Place leather sheet in a drying tray and dry at 135 degrees until rhubarb is hard. Place dried rhubarb in a bowl and crush with your hands to make flakes.

The advantage of drying is to eliminate the water so that you can use rhubarb in ways otherwise impossible or difficult.

Recipe Index